FIVE STEPS TO SPIRITUAL GROWTH

FIVE STEPS TO SPIRITUAL GROWTH

⤎ A *Journey* ⤏

Peter M. Kalellis

Paulist Press
New York/Mahwah, N.J.

Cover design by Trudi Gershenov
Book design by Lynn Else

Library of Congress Cataloging-in-Publication Data

Kalellis, Peter M.
    Five steps to spiritual growth : a journey / Peter M. Kalellis.
        p. cm.
    Includes bibliographical references.
    ISBN 0-8091-4302-X (alk. paper)
    1. Spiritual formation. I. Title.

    BV4511.K25 2005
    248.4—dc22

                                                                    2004020936

Published by Paulist Press
997 Macarthur Boulevard
Mahwah, New Jersey 07430

www.paulistpress.com

Printed and bound in the
United States of America

Contents

STEP FIVE: THE ULTIMATE REALITY

This book is lovingly dedicated

To Pat, my wonderful wife and caring companion,
who often reminds me that having fun
and maintaining a balanced life
is an integral part of spirituality.

To my loving children Katina, Michael and Mercene,
whose lives I have tried to direct toward
the Giver of all blessings.

To the newlyweds, my son Basil and his wife Yen Fen,
with all good wishes for a long and happy life.
May God continue to bestow his blessings
on their spiritual journey.

To all my readers who are seeking a more meaningful life.

Acknowledgments

An intimate relationship evolves between the author and his book. Much is required of the author—availability, commitment, faith, discipline, and diligence. These qualities are all fine and good, but they are not sufficient for the actual material of a book. One needs external resources to test personal concepts and obtain feedback. In the process of writing, I involved several friends who helped sustain my enthusiasm, challenged my ideas, and improved my approach in appealing to a broad spectrum of readers.

Wendell Shackelford, who has enormous experience both in writing and in the publishing field, has consistently and patiently proven himself to be a most valuable mentor and a genuine friend over a period of thirty years.

Margery Hueston deserves a whole page of thanks for her patience and her ever-meticulous contribution in giving form and shape to my manuscripts since my first attempts at becoming an author.

Demetria DeLia and Monica Metta, friends and colleagues in the healing arts, whose lives are dedicated to an untiring effort to relieve human pain, provided inspiration to complete this book.

Among the many faithful friends who offer encouragement for my writing projects, I would like to thank Ernie Anastos, Michelle LePoidevin, Joseph Goldman, Joan Petrakis, Frank

Esposito, Susan Thul, Norman Brosniak, Nadia Ansary, Theodore Kalmoukos, Arleen Terpening, and Laura Tharny.

For their faith and trust in my work, I express special gratitude to the most reverend archbishops: Maximos of Pittsburgh, Pennsylvania, Anthony of San Francisco, California, Methodios of Boston, Massachusetts, Alexis of Atlanta, Georgia, and Evangelos of New Jersey; and appreciation is extended to the reverend clergy: Sarantos Serviou, Theo Anastos, James Dokos, Angelo Gavalas, Anthony Pappas, Jerry Hall, Paul Kucynda, Nicholas Pathenos, Demetrios Kavadas, George Poulos, and Anthony Coniaris. They have graced my life with love and moral support.

Words of heartfelt appreciation and thanks are expressed also to the editors and publisher for the printing and final production of this book.

Prologue

I had planned to write this book later in my life when my maturity, clarity of mind, and self-confidence were developed and synchronized. After several requests, it seemed I had no choice but to tackle the task, although I felt inadequate in dealing with issues of faith. The writing brought me face to face with myself, so that by the time the manuscript was completed, I had engaged in thorough self-analysis, self-evaluation, self-discipline, and trust in Jesus Christ, the king of kings and perfecter of life.

As the writing progressed, my feelings of inadequacy increased. I struggled with my own spirituality. *Am I spiritual enough? Do I have the backbone to carry out such a sensitive theme? What qualifies me to undertake this project?* The process, far from being an intellectual endeavor to impress the reader, required commitment, constant prayer, and self-scrutiny. My resistances kept rising, as I realized that spirituality—beneficial and essential as it may be—is an intricate issue to bring into a materially saturated world. I wondered how I could make it clear and viable for the reader, without sounding dogmatic or rigid. Further, in the demanding society in which we live, where people work hard to meet their practical needs, when time for serious thought is limited, when evenings are consumed by television, the subject of spirituality needs to be delineated so that it may be understood, and that is not a simple matter.

It is a reality that from childhood to adulthood to old age, we all go through physical and emotional transformations. During these stages, something special and good is growing inside us. We need to provide proper sunshine and nourishment to ensure that it grows in health and vigor. At the same time, we live in a state of tension between two realities: First, the world endangers our existence, tempting us with promises of happiness and demanding our obedience to its rules. Second, we are aware of the supernatural existence of God for whom, even unknowingly, we yearn. This divine being calls forth beyond the laws and boundaries of our life to the service of a spiritual life that starts here on earth and continues in God's eternal kingdom.

Encouragement and moral support did come to me from a number of people who had read my previous book, *Restoring Your Self: Five Ways Toward a Healthier, Happier, and More Creative Life.* The callers were of different religious orientations; several claimed to be agnostics. Their urge to contact me was precipitated by the *Fifth Way,* the final part of the book that deals with *Self-Transformation,* an invitation to pursue a spiritual approach to life. As I talked with these readers, I became increasingly aware of the deep-seated human need for spiritual guidance and, of course, my own personal need for spiritual renewal. So, with humility and respect, and gratitude to God for inspiring me to write about spirituality, I laid the foundation for this book in *Step One: Your Inner Journey.*

As you read the pages that follow, please ascend each of the *Five Steps* carefully and slowly. This is a heartfelt invitation, offering a reliable guide to assist you in your spiritual journey. It is not a portrait of personal wisdom; it is not a course to convert the reader. Simply, it is an earnest effort and reliable mentoring inspired by the unique personality of Jesus Christ our Lord and the exemplary life of his followers.

If you wish to develop your spiritual life, the time is now. During this reading allow yourself to absorb what makes sense to you. Do not try to speed-read this book in the way you might read a novel. Discuss what stands out in your mind about the book with a dear friend. Talking to a friend or to a religious person about your gleanings of this effort could make for an interesting conversation and a meaningful relationship. Keep in mind that a major goal of spiritual life is to harvest and enjoy the *fruit of the Spirit, which is love, joy, peace, patience, kindness, generosity, faithfulness, gentleness, and self-control* (Gal 5:22). These qualities are the gift of the Holy Spirit, inherent in every human being.

Peter M. Kalellis

Foreword

Five Steps to Spiritual Growth: A Journey is a significant book whose intention is to point out the value of a human being, God's unique creation. Written in flowing language, the book helps a person—in spite of his or her past experience—to visualize the reality of present and future.

Dr. Peter Kalellis has explored and gleaned aspects of spiritual life as experienced by personalities of early church history, and with simplicity he introduces spirituality to today's reader as an attainable lifestyle.

The theme permeating the book is that humans are not just physical; they are spiritual beings by God's design. Awareness and effort to develop their own spirituality make life physically healthier and mentally happier. The author assists readers to ascend each step with a feeling of relief that God is always present in their lives, accepting, loving, forgiving sins and unwitting errors. The spiritual ascent becomes easier and smoother as we remove obstacles of destructive habits, evil thoughts, and negativity. Abundant love and tender mercy, wisdom and direction are God's gifts. They are not imposed on anyone; one needs to be willing to receive them, and then the rest of the ascent becomes his work.

Today, professionals in the healing arts, including psychiatrists, psychotherapists, marriage family therapists, and social workers recognize how spiritual people regain their physical and emotional health faster than others who have no religious affiliation.

Having read Dr. Kalellis's previous book, *Restoring Your Self: Five Ways to a Healthier, Happier, and More Creative Life*, I was particularly impressed by part 5, which deals with *Self–Transformation*. I had a hunch another book was in the air. I am now delighted to see it in print: *Five Steps to Spiritual Growth: A Journey*. In these adverse times, when the media portray the Hollywood lifestyle as reality, our homes are inundated with news of terror and insecurity, and advertisements promote goods that promise happiness but leave the consumer in deep debt—and in dire need of something different, something worthwhile, something fulfilling—this book will take you on a journey that offers something solid and different.

The author provides easy-to-follow directives and allows readers to reconsider existent—perhaps dormant and healthy—qualities that are inner human properties that can be applied effectively. Truly, this book does enrich the ascent of each step with insights and valuable material that, put into practice, will bring peace of mind, direction in life, strength, and wisdom to anyone who chooses to accept the offerings.

Michelle H. LePoidevin, Editor
*The Westfield Leader and the Times—
Scotch Plains–Fanwood, New Jersey*

Step One

Your Inner Journey

As you begin the inward journey, three areas require your attention:

First, check and clarify your present position—seek out events that took place over the years and caused you to be who you are today.

Second, think about the importance of your destination and evaluate it.

Third, prepare yourself adequately. No heavy luggage is necessary. This journey can prove to be a new beginning, a lasting joy. It requires only sound faith, focus, and a desire to learn about God's presence in the world and in your personal life.

Chapter 1

A New Beginning

We must learn to live each day, each hour,
each minute as a new beginning, as a unique
opportunity to make everything new.
The past and the future keep harassing us.
The past with guilt, the future with worries.

Henri J. M. Nouwen

This inner journey that you are taking presently requires attention and preparation. Unlike your other travels when you had to carry baggage, this inner journey does not require physical effort on your part, for no material belongings are needed. The only necessity you must have is a genuine desire for a *newness of life*. The goal is to become a better person in the eyes of God.

A sensitive assessment of your life will indicate that you have to understand and follow the guidelines that will best help you to attain peace of mind and soul, which, in turn, point you in the direction of ultimate human destiny, reunion with God. This means an awareness of God's presence and purpose in your life.

Different religions offer their ethical codes, teachings, and rules to guide people toward God. Christians and Jews commonly share the Ten Commandments. Christians have the gospel to guide and measure their conduct. Buddhists follow the eightfold path of Dharma (Truth/Law); Hindus, Muslims, and other groups have similar frameworks. While their objective is of great benefit—to relieve each population of its misery and pre-occupation with materialism—how the principles of any faith are applied in daily living is a major issue. All human beings around the world have similar needs. They want to be accepted, loved, and respected. They want to have a decent life, one of freedom, health, and material prosperity. However, these needs can be significantly forged by faith in God, the provider and sustainer of the universe, the true God who loves you personally and wishes happiness for you.

It is not the intention of this book to provide a global solution that could be applied to everyone's spiritual needs. Essentially, this book is designed to help you develop a personal spiritual direction that will make sense in your present life. It is to reassure you that nothing can separate you from the love of God, and that knowledge of God's love will give you lasting joy. This gift is yours because of your faith.

My faith is weak. I have doubts. I was never a believer; it's too late to start now. My past is mired with mistakes and sins I have committed.

A good start is to make peace with your past. *My past is a painful nightmare,* you might say bitterly. To that, I can only reply, *We cannot change the past; we can only change our attitude about it and live a clean life. Bear in mind that saints have a past also, but sinners have a future.*

The Bible has preserved portraits—mired by sins and violations—of personalities whose lives changed dramatically when, having admitted they had done wrong, they sought forgiveness and accepted God's unconditional love. In summary, here are a few examples:

David the king of Israel committed two major crimes: adultery and murder. When his kingdom began to collapse, Nathan the prophet pointed out to David that the deterioration was a result of his sins. One might have expected David to be arrogant and say, *I'm the king. I know what I'm doing.* Such was not the case; David did not rationalize his style of life or minimize its seriousness. He was full of regret; he acknowledged his guilt and asked for God's help. How striking are the lines of Psalm 51, one of David's many psalms:

> *Have mercy on me, O God, because of Your unfailing love. Because of Your great compassion, remove the stain of my sins. I recognize my shameful deeds—they haunt me day and night. Against You, and You alone, have I sinned; I have done evil in Your sight.*
>
> *Purify me of my sins, and I will be clean; wash me, and I will be whiter than snow. Oh, give me back my joy again. Restore in me the joy of your salvation.*

The gospel story of the prodigal son encapsulates God's abundant love to the one who repents and changes conduct. Having spent his portion of inheritance in loose living, with prostitutes and drunkards, the prodigal son returned to his father's home. His sorrowful heart and soul cried: *Father I have sinned before heaven and before you, and I am no longer worthy to be called your son. Treat me as one of your hired servants.* His compassionate father embraced him and kissed him affectionately and ordered a celebration to be given for his son's return. How eloquently the gospels claim that *great joy takes place in heaven, and the angels rejoice, when a sinner changes his mind.*

The poignant life of St. Paul the apostle is worthy of consideration. St. Paul saw himself as a faithful Jew, loyal to a great and sacred heritage, a person who had a duty to crush the followers of Christ:

> *I myself was convinced that I ought to do many things in opposing the name of Jesus. And I did so in Jerusalem. When his followers were put to death, I cast my vote against them...and in raging fury against them, I pursued them even to foreign cities.*

Actually, for Paul, jailing and killing Christians was a last resort; he had tried, and failed, to get them to renounce Jesus — in his words, *to make them blaspheme.*

After his personal experience in Damascus, a self-transformation, he became a fervent follower of Christ. Diligently, Paul reordered his previous lifestyle. For repentance and self-discipline, he spent three years in the desert of Arabia. There in silence and solitude, he totally surrendered to the will of his master. He suffered anguish over his past violations: *I am the least of the apostles, unfit to be called an apostle, because I persecuted the Church of God.* To right his wrongs and to praise his beloved master, he took on a lifetime commitment to preach the gospel of truth and justice, words of love and reconciliation, which are preserved in his epistles.

The evident joy that St. Paul experienced once he made a turn in his life is eloquently expressed in his epistle to the people of Philippi, Greece:

Rejoice in the Lord always; again I will say, Rejoice. Let your gentleness be known to everyone. The Lord is near. Do not worry about anything, but in everything by prayer and thanksgiving let your requests be made known to God. And the peace of God, which surpasses all understanding, will guard your hearts and your minds. Beloved brothers and sisters, whatever is true, whatever is honorable, whatever is just, whatever is pure, whatever is pleasing, whatever is commendable, if there is any excellence and if there is anything worthy of praise, think and keep doing these things...and the God of peace will be with you.

This brief admonition is a result of St. Paul's new life, and it may be a good start for a person who is considering a new direction in life. Truly, you and I cannot be St. Paul, and it is not expected of us. Yet, if we have a bad behavior record, if we have a nagging past, we can let go of it, but we cannot change it. What we can change is our attitude toward our past and conceivably consider God's forgiveness.

As we explore the human potential for a spiritual direction in life, the stories of Mary Magdalene and Mary of Egypt attract our attention.

Both women became prostitutes early in life. A raging crowd with handfuls of stones was eager to kill Mary Magdalene, for she had committed adultery. But her life turned around when Jesus appeared on the scene and said, *Let the one that has no sin cast the first stone*. As her accusers, one by one, disappeared, he said, *Where are your accusers? Go and sin no more*. From that moment, Mary Magdalene's life changed. She became a fervent follower of Jesus, and she was the first to witness his resurrection.

Mary of Egypt lived and worked in a brothel for seventeen years. To pay for her passage from Alexandria to Jerusalem, she sold her body to a group of lusty sailors. In her words, *I do not have the fare, but I have a beautiful body, as you see, and you can do whatever you want with it*. The sailors took her aboard, and what they did with her on the boat one can only imagine.

In Jerusalem, as she attempted to enter the Church of Resurrection, an inner force held her back. She could not take a step forward. After profound self-scrutiny, gnawing guilt paralyzed her. *It devastates me still to remember that, even on such a holy journey, I corrupted many of the pilgrims.* She cried endlessly about her former life and sought God's mercy. Wholeheartedly, she repented and accepted God's unconditional love and forgiveness.

The Church of the East and West venerates these two Marys as saints and portrays them as models of *metanoia*, changing mind, and following a healthier direction in life. History has preserved countless personalities who initially lived a prodigal and sinful life, but at a certain point, realizing their deterioration and feeling regret about their violations, they decided to seek a better direction.

The above examples point out one major reality. Once a person makes a decision to start a spiritual life, he or she feels empowered by God's grace of forgiveness and unconditional acceptance. As you meditate on the whole concept of divine love and forgiveness, it is important to realize that God does not divide people according to their virtues or vices, but according to their honest desire to accept the grace that he offers them. He does not justify or condone wrongdoing, but he rewards repentance. God offers pardon to the person who admits his violations and wrongs, who understands that he has gone astray, and who now has regrets.

The realities of life confirm what St. Paul said, *All have sinned and come short of the glory of God* (Rom 3:23). But God wants all humans to be saved from their sins and become aware of the truth that brings about joy and peace of mind.

Psychotherapists who deal with troubled lives more often than not encounter clients whose lives wallow in trouble: adultery, betrayal, embezzlement, infidelity, incest, lies, theft, violence, and so forth. The fact that a person resorts to psychotherapy indicates that the inner part, the soul, is suffering and is yearning for relief. If such a client connects with a seasoned therapist who understands that the emotional ailments are symptoms of a suffering soul, the client may make significant progress. Healing begins when the therapist taps not simply on the presenting problems, which could be pain-evoking, but also explores the spiritual dimension of a human being.

In the process of divorcing her third husband, Deborah, a stunning woman of exceptional talents, developed a multimillion dollar business in fashion design. Rapidly, she had ascended the ladder of success, not always with legitimate transactions. In her early forties, blonde and beautiful, with a diamond-studded cross hanging from her gold necklace, she thought nothing of violating certain rules. *The end justifies the means,* she told herself. *Besides, in my company, many individuals and families make a handsome living.* She claimed to be a good Christian and contributed generously to her church, which she attended faithfully.

Deborah became severely depressed. Sleepless nights, loss of weight, no motivation, irritability—all took a toll on her. Even her employees noticed the change in her and began to feel insecure and became less productive. When the IRS investigated her records for tax evasion, she fell off the deep end. She owed enormous amounts of money, and she had to sell her company. The ancient proverb, *The liar and the thief rejoice the first years, but they spend the last years in jail,* proved to be true in Deborah's case. Yet, while her appearance remained inviolate, her violations caught up with her and caused deep inner turmoil. The antidepressants took the edge off for a little while, but in her therapy, she came to realize her wrong perceptions of life on both personal and business levels. *I must have a hole in my soul,* she admitted.

"What do you mean?" I asked.

"Somehow, the values I grew up with, the Christian principles that my parents taught me must have gone through me."

While she was serving a year's sentence in jail, she confessed to a chaplain: *Ambition, greed, and lust have brought me here. I need a change in my life.* A victim of her choices, Deborah was looking for a new direction.

Thoughts to Consider:

- No matter who you are and what you have done in your life, waste no more time thinking of your past. If there is a way that you can make amends, such as restoring damages, do it in the spirit of humility. Your greatest challenge is you. Embrace yourself, accept what you have or what you have left in your life and make a new beginning.

- Stop judging yourself. Instead of anxiously ruminating on the past, choose to let it go and enjoy the present, each day, each hour. Be fully present where you are and in what you do. Learn to appreciate the good around you. Take time to smell the roses, to laugh with friends, to enjoy meals together, and, above all, celebrate God's presence in your life.

- Don't compromise with the thought, *I'm only human; what else can I expect of myself? What if things don't work out?* This is the understatement of your life. You are not only human—you are also divine in potential. There is a space within you where your soul dwells. Enter that space. The fulfillment of all your goals and aspirations in life depends upon connecting with your soul and releasing more of that divine potential.

Chapter 2

Faith—The Anchor of Hope

*Faith is sureness of spiritual truth, of that which is or
of God; of the existence of the spiritual world with all
its properties, similarly as we are sure of the material
world with all the things that belong to it.*

John Sergiev of Kronstadt
(Russian mystic)

Faith is a necessary ingredient for a spiritual life. Everyday
life requires some faith that points us in the direction we should
go. Making a decision implies we have faith in the goal we want
to pursue. Faith is believing—in a person, a place, an idea, or a
system—either without proof or before anticipated results are
delivered. Sometimes we see results, but often we end up frustrated because results are delayed or denied.

Perhaps at one time you prayed to God to relieve you from
suffering or to help you with a personal problem, and it is possible you did not experience any special result. This does not
mean that God did not hear your prayers. His delay is not a
denial. If your faith is focused in a God of love, an extraordinary
power that can help to bring about your desired wish will be
unleashed in your mind. The power of faith is not exclusively a
religious phenomenon. It can be a strong trust in anyone or anything, and it is uniquely a personal experience.

You may have seen children jumping into the arms of their parents. They have total and unconditional trust and faith that loving arms will catch them and protect them from danger. The first time I saw a trapeze artist, I was fascinated by the daring and risky performer. The artist who let go of his swing had full confidence that his counterpart would receive him. Of course, human doubt played its part — a safety net was in place in case of an accident. Faith in God requires total trust; we need no external support, because the caring father is at the other end to receive us when we take that leap of faith.

Faith is a faculty of the soul that finds its most perfect expression among spiritual people. In order to manifest its complete character, faith must be developed in all its phases. Endowed with faith, human beings magnify their strength, their courage, and their power. History informs us of the initial triumphs of Christianity. Great achievements were accomplished as a result of unwavering faith. In the midst of a cruel pagan world, a small group of obscure individuals, the apostles with faith in their master, reached out and spoke the truth about God's caring love and righteousness.

In the eleventh chapter of the Epistle to the Hebrews, the author gives a concise definition of faith: *Faith is the assurance of things hoped for, the conviction of things "that exist" yet not seen.* In the latter part of the same chapter, the author vividly describes what believers in his time were able to accomplish and endure:

> *Through their faith they conquered kingdoms, administered justice, obtained promises, shut the mouths of lions, extinguished raging fire, escaped the edge of the*

sword, won strength out of weakness, became mighty in war, put foreign armies to flight. Women received their dead by resurrection. Others were tortured, suffered mocking and flogging. They were stoned to death, they were sawn in two, they were killed by the sword; they went about in skins of sheep and goats, destitute, persecuted, tormented—yet though they were commended for their faith, did not receive what was promised, since God had promised something better.

With faith in God's promise, successors of the apostles like Ignatius of Antioch and Polycarp of Smyrna, in their effort to safeguard the teaching of Christ, suffered martyrdom in the early part of the second century. They had learned about Christ from John the evangelist, and because of their unwavering faith, they were sentenced to death. Ignatius was thrown to the lions, and Polycarp was burned alive. Fragments of their writings continue to echo in our times; their faith nurtures our souls.

In part of a letter to his friends in Rome who wanted to mitigate his sentence, Ignatius said:

I respect your good will and charity...for it is easy for you to do what you please; but it is difficult for me to come to God unless you hold back your hands. I shall never have an opportunity of reaching my Lord. Therefore, now that the altar is ready, let me offer myself to Him. Permit me to be the food of wild beasts through whom I may attain God. I am God's grain, and I am to be ground by the teeth of wild beasts that

I may be found the pure bread of Christ. Entice the lions to become my sepulcher that they may leave nothing of my body. Excuse me in this matter. I know what is good for me.

May nothing visible or invisible prevent me from attaining my Lord. Come fire and cross, gashes and rendings, breaking of bones and mangling of limbs, the shattering of pieces of my whole body; come all the wicked torments of the devil upon me but let me be in the presence of my Lord.

As the Roman soldiers were about to start the pyre and burn Polycarp, Nero the emperor offered him a last chance. "If you reject your faith in Christ and pay tribute to Caesar, you don't have to die." Humbly, Polycarp answered: "Eighty-six years I have served my Lord and he never did me wrong, how can I reject him or blaspheme against my king who is the author of my life?"

"Start the fire," shouted Herod. Smoke and flames enveloped Polycarp's body, but his final words could be heard clearly. "Lord God Almighty, blessed and praised be your holy name. Thank you for accepting me into your kingdom, through Jesus Christ, your beloved Son." The moment he said, *Christ, your beloved Son,* one of the executioners angrily plunged his sword into Polycarp's side.

As we meditate on biblical verses or on the lives of the early martyrs, we realize that the true heroes of life are not necessarily the triumphant victors. The ones who might appear defeated could be the real heroes, because their faith promises a ray of hope. We should remind ourselves that God always provides something better for us. That is the way God works. One of the most exciting things in life is the realization that our soul's greatest yearning is to know more about him and his plans for us. There is simply nothing as satisfying as the knowledge of who God is and what he is like. "No one has ever seen God, except the one who came down from heaven," said Christ. "If you have seen me, you have seen God the Father."

As we believe and unconditionally accept his plan of salvation by reading the gospel and pondering it in our hearts, we discover God. And knowing God gives us a sense of inner peace and strength. That inner transformation is God's work. The indwelling of the Holy Spirit is active from the time of our baptism, ever chiseling off human passions and ever restoring in us the image of God. *"Let us make humankind in our image, according to our likeness"* (Gen 1:26). As we draw closer to him we will realize, no matter what is happening in our life, that he will provide a solution. As we go through stormy days, he is there to lead us to calmer seas. Henri J. M. Nouwen observes:

> *The great spiritual challenge is to discover, over time, that the limited, conditional, and temporal love we receive from parents, husbands, wives, children, teachers, colleagues, and friends are reflections of the unlimited, unconditional, everlasting love of God. Whenever we can make that huge leap of faith, we will know that death is no longer the end but the gateway to the fullness of the Divine Love.*

The moment we make God a reality in our lives and see him as a benevolent force that holds all things together, we notice that even without our conscious control we are fully alive.

Consider the physical self. Our body is at work every moment, functioning with an array of intricate interacting mechanisms that make life possible. Our minds perceive experiences and ideas, our eyes see, our hearts beat, our lungs breathe, our ears hear, our hair grows—the whole physical apparatus is at work with efficiency that our human efforts cannot match. Of course, we fuel the mechanism with food, but what happens when we eat? After chewing and swallowing, the enzymes take over to help the digestion and distribute the nutrients to all the organs of the body. Beneath the surface of our physical form is a heart that beats a lifetime, a mind active around the clock, and a defense mechanism—the immune system—that makes the U.S. defense system look like a child's toy; billions of cells work harmoniously together. What power makes this process possible?

The natural world evokes our attention and challenges our faith. Planets revolve around the sun, seeds become flowers and trees. The whole concept of conception is astounding: The seed meets the egg, becomes an embryo, and eventually a baby. All these creations, events, and movements that we take for granted are built into a harmonious system sustained by an external force. Our attempts to direct this force would put us in jeopardy. To trust this force, to believe that all is well because the force governs and protects us—that is what we can call *faith*.

Consider the yearning of the soul, the part of you that wants to know God. Our willingness to relax into this force allows it to work on our behalf for our physical, emotional, and spiritual wellness. In our search for spirituality, unconditional faith in God is necessary. As the infant finds comfort and warmth in the loving arms of its mother, likewise maturing people have the choice of surrendering to the arms of a caring God to find love and serenity. This is an act of faith.

Surrender may seem unrealistic to you, even scary. You may have doubts about your ability to surrender. It is of vital importance to place yourself in God's loving care, to feel his presence in your life and his involvement in the affairs of humanity, to desire his truth, and to seek his ultimate plan for you. As you meditate on the word *surrender*, you may discover that it is an activity of your soul. It is with the eyes of the soul that we see clearly the way life is; accept it and be true to it whatever the pain, because the pain of not being true to it is far greater.

Humans, endowed with reason and the power of abstract thought, employ faith as a substitute for exact knowledge in their effort to interpret the meaning and the value of life. When they begin to penetrate beneath the surface of things, to look beyond the facts of immediate experience, in the absence of tangible evidence, it is faith that supplies the inspiration and the courage to go ahead.

In scientific research as well as in philosophical thought, faith must be relied upon to provide the realities not present in the conscious mind. Faith is the master key to great discoveries, inventions. and achievements. There are always unknown factors or qualities that must be accepted on faith to complete a solution, a structure, a design. In the healing arts we have many and varied systems of securing health, but all of them depend upon faith for their effectiveness.

Christ, the great healer, emphasized that faith was a necessary requisite of cure. *Your faith has made you well,* he said to the afflicted, and they regained their health instantly. Faith cannot be described as being artificial, blind, or credulous, nor is it synonymous with merely ordinary belief. Belief is an activity of the intellect, but faith is the fruit of the soul.

In his affirmation, *If you have faith the size of a mustard seed you will say to this mountain, "Move from here to there," and it will move; and nothing will be impossible for you* (Matt 17:20), Christ reassures us of the immeasurable power of faith. When we transcend the limits of our being and focus our faith on the giver of life in whose divine presence we are, we will become aware of the change that occurs within. The apostle Paul said to the Athenians, *In Him we live and move and have our being* (Acts 17:28). As we incorporate and blend our lives with the exemplary life of Christ, we become transformed, empowered, and enriched.

As we walk the path of our gradual transformation, we need to be careful not to be puffed up by pride, *the holier than thou* precept. If pride prevails because we believe that we are the right kind of people, then we detach ourselves from the rest of humanity, succumb to the fear of losing control, and find ourselves lonely. Genuine faith implies that we reach out toward others to help, to share, to appreciate their presence, and to interact with them in a mutually beneficial way. As we aim for a reciprocal validation, we sense the joy of belonging to each other. Only through our capacity to believe in others do our personalities reach their fullest and highest state of development. In all human contacts and relationships, faith is the keynote to success.

In the home, the community, the nation, and the world at large, faith in the people concerned is indispensable in securing lasting harmony, understanding, peace, and happiness.

A light bulb is nothing more than that until it is turned on. When the connection is made with electrical energy, it becomes a radiant source of light and warmth. Humans are spiritual beings, children of God, heirs to all the infinite potential inherent in all God's creation, including love, the strongest single force in existence. But in reality, the fulfilling of the power of our soul comes only when we are attuned to our Lord God and are expressing his love, light, and power.

Humans are creatures of light. At any time and under any circumstances, you and I can switch on the light to dissolve darkness. Christ defined the purpose of our existence in a brief statement: *You are the light of the world....Let your light shine before others, so that they may see your works and give glory to your Father in heaven* (Matt 5:14). Faith is the deep trust that God's love is stronger than all the powers of the world; such trust transforms us from victims of darkness to servants of light. Having God's light in our hearts, we can reach out and enlighten other people. We can extend our love to help and heal broken relationships, awaken hearts, heal wounds, and become a beneficial presence in the life of others.

One cannot find real joy in love that does not also encompass faith. Romantic love may constitute the motive and the basis of many marriages, but the essence of faith is a unique ingredient in assuring permanency. Without the abiding trust, the home becomes but a dwelling place built upon the foundations of shifting sand. Faith is the bond that perpetuates human under-standing and friendship.

Thoughts to Consider:

- Crises are part of human affairs. The world is confused and afraid. Homes and families are inundated with conflicting information on how to live their lives. You may be facing a crucial period in your life that requires a viable solution. The remedy is in the hands of God. He has the wisdom and power to alleviate the sufferings of the world. Faith and trust in his will is a promising choice.

- Try to make God a reality in your life, and try to see him as a working force in your daily life. This mystical connection between you and God will enable you to encounter life with strength and courage, in spite of opposing forces and adversities you encounter.

- The experience of faith is a choice we make; it is a mental decision to see faith as the strongest value in any situation. To stop analyzing and relax, to feel the faith in your heart and keep it as your tool in every situation—that's a firm step toward your spirituality and a more rewarding life.

Chapter 3

God—The Author of Life

I believe in One God, the Father Almighty, Maker of
heaven and earth, and of all things visible and invisible.
Nicean Creed AD 325

This chapter invites the readers to confirm their own faith
in one God who is the Creator, who rules and sustains the universe, and is in charge of our lives. Human thought alone arrives
at the belief that God exists. However, the truth of God is not
perceived by the mind alone. If the finite human mind could
define God, the definition would be limited and confined to
human needs, fears, and desires. Being that God is immaterial,
there can be no scientific proof of his existence. We do not see
God with our physical eyes. If we do not see something, does that
mean it does not exist? Can we see electricity? We see its results:
light and power. Can we see the air? We breathe; we know it is
indispensable to life, and, as we move, we sense its existence.

As science evolves, we continually discover that what our
senses perceive is but an infinitesimal part of reality. That is why
the existence of God can never be fully proven or disproven.
This is also true with regard to the incomprehensible power that
created the world. It is with the eyes of faith that we can see
God. It is with a heart of love and devotion that we can learn
about the author of life and death. Faith in God requires an act

of will to believe. It is a matter of faith whether one believes in God or believes that everything visible came into being by itself or by chance.

If nothing in this world can be created spontaneously, of its own accord, how could the whole universe have been created by itself? If even a glass cannot be filled with water by its own power, how could the world have been filled by its own power with wonders from galaxies to germs, from planets to planet earth with its abundance of life, and from stars to human minds? The conclusion is evident to the reader. Faith takes us from things that are within reason to things that are above reason.

It is true that atheism is more a result of intensive propaganda and less a result of logic. Even in our times, some pundits claim that there is no God. One may wonder: Is their claim a power issue, an ego trip to prove their superiority as thinkers, or is their claim rooted in a covert fear that their unethical and perverted behavior will be revealed? Their purpose may aim to uproot faith in God from the heart of their listeners or readers in order to provide a "supposed" unconditional freedom to do whatever feels good. But what happens to those who are influenced by atheistic notions? They resemble people who have had one leg amputated, but who do not refute the fact that humans are two-legged beings; the atheist undermines the truth that humans are by nature religious beings.

In the midst of scientific evolution, Nietzsche proclaimed: *God is dead.* It is important, however, to realize that the God he thought science had killed, the God who was no longer compatible with rational thinking, was the personal Creator God of the

Bible. There is nothing in science or reason to refute the concept of this higher and mystical reality of God's presence in the world.

Explorers and researchers have found primitive races isolated on remote islands of the Pacific and in the virgin forests of Africa who not only have some form of religion but also have a clear idea of a Supreme Being, a Creator and Sustainer of the Universe, who is good and who rewards humans according to their deeds.

Some may insist that ancient and primitive peoples believed out of fear and ignorance. That could have been partially true in early human history, but what can we say today when ignorance has been diminished? God is not necessarily the product of a cognitive process. He is, instead, "discovered" in a mystical or spiritual encounter made known through meditation and prayer. It is only with a spirit of reverence that a person can begin to understand God, who cannot be put in a box or laid out in a laboratory to be dissected. Should someone try this small-minded approach, it is not God that he dissects, but his own illusion.

Simply, humans do not cognitively invent an almighty God and then depend upon their invention to gain the feeling of control. God is spiritually experienced in the life of believers. People who intimately believe in God feel the security of his presence everywhere. If we trust our perceptions of the physical world that surrounds us, we have no rational reason to claim that our concept of a Creator is a condition of the mind. Faith in the power and wisdom of a loving God offers believers the assurance that their lives have meaning and purpose. They are not alone in the struggle for survival, and despite the adversities of life, they should not feel afraid.

Present scientific research leads to God, whose will and wisdom are also revealed in natural laws. Observations made in the past together with investigations of the present prove that devoutness is a general characteristic of the human race, and atheism is an abnormal and morbid condition. Study and knowledge, not ignorance, strengthen our belief in God. Never before has the historical and universal evidence of God's existence been so well confirmed as it is today.

The spacecraft Apollo 15 made a journey to the moon in 1971. Aboard was astronaut James Irwin, who spoke to us from space:

I can't describe to you the thrill of looking out into space and seeing it as only a handful of men have ever seen it. Of seeing the sun and stars in the most brilliant, breathtaking colors mankind has ever witnessed.

And then to look in another direction, and there hanging like a multicolored, luminous, giant marble was earth. I could hardly contain myself.

I came to a stop. Moon dust settled down on my boots and chills ran up and down my spine. I thought "Wow! This is the greatest miracle in the human race. Man is walking on the moon!"

Then God spoke to my heart: "No, Jim, it isn't really. The greatest miracle in the history of mankind is not that man walked on the moon; it's that God walks on the earth and lives in you."

In her book, *A History of God*, Karen Armstrong points out that the presence of God has made profoundly positive contributions to Western culture:

> *The personal God has helped monotheists to value the sacred and inalienable rights of the individual and to develop an appreciation of human personality.*

Believers who are connected with their personal God feel validated. *I'm important in God's eyes. I'm here for a purpose. God has a plan for me.* Such a trend of thought lifts them out of fear and futility. Believing that God is in charge of life, they experience confidence and motivation for daily existence.

Although the essence of God is beyond human comprehension, in the early days, people of faith and devotion, in the spirit of reverence, began to understand God. They relied upon intense prayer, fasting, silence, and various forms of mortification to free their minds from mundane matters and focus more intently on God. In his limited way, John of Damascus (675–749), a monk of the East, says:

> *Now we both know and confess that God is without beginning and without end, everlasting and eternal, uncreated, unchangeable...invisible, unfathomable, good, just, the maker of all created things.*

John's affirmation grows more specific, when he adds:

> *We furthermore know and confess that God is one, that is to say one in essence and inseparable. He is both*

understood to be and is three in Persons—I mean the
Father and the Son and the Holy Spirit.

This concept of God as a Trinity united in one without division is the point where human understanding and language find their limit. The truth of the Trinity comes to us from the Book of Genesis 1:26. As God is about to create Adam and Eve, he says: *Let us make humankind.* The plural *let us make* implies that God is not alone in his creative form. God the Father commands the word, God the Son creates, and God the Holy Spirit gives life to the creation.

In the New Testament, the Trinity is initially revealed at the Jordan River when Christ was baptized. At that time, as the Son entered the river, the Holy Spirit in the form of a dove soared over him, and the voice of the Father resounded from heaven: *This is my Beloved Son.* Finally, the truth about one God in Three Persons was confirmed by Christ's command to the apostles after his resurrection: *Go and teach all nations, baptizing them in the name of the Father, and of the Son, and of the Holy Spirit* (Matt 28:19).

In our skepticism, it may be difficult to discern spiritual realities from rational thinking. The concept of the Holy Trinity is a mystery, and to aid our inquisitive minds, we use comparisons from nature: Water can be perceived in three forms—as liquid, ice, and vapor. A shamrock consists of three leaves joined to one stem. The sun may represent the Father, the sun's rays the Son, the sun's light the Holy Spirit. These are only human images of divine realities.

Gregory the Theologian (330–389), a man of piety and prayer, concludes:

> I have very carefully considered this matter of the Triune God in my own mind and soul, and have looked at it from every point of view in order to find some likeness of this mystery, but I have been unable to discover anything on earth with which to compare the nature of the Godhead.

Although the essence of God is ultimately unattainable for the human mind, the existence of God is real and active in each moment of life. Nothing has been created that was not created by God. He is everywhere present. God is the ever-flowing source of power and creativity, the foundation and father of all creation, the giver of all knowledge and all perfect gifts, who loves and cares for us, for we are his children.

The aim of spirituality is for us to come close to God, communion or union with God, that we may be part of his blessings: *Where is God that I may come close to him*, you may ask. The answer is, *he is already close to you*.

God wants to be allowed into our lives. But in our quest as consumers for the latest gadgets, fast cars, elegant homes, prestigious jobs, exotic vacations, early retirement fantasies, we virtually negate the inner life. Surrounded by intense noises caused by our mechanized living style and external voices that influence our lives, we cannot hear God's voice: *I am the Lord your God; consecrate yourselves therefore, and be holy, for I am holy* (Lev 11:44).

Maximus the Confessor (580–662) said: *A human being is called to become by divine grace all that God Himself is by nature.* This simply means that God wills and helps his children to be like he is, and that is the purpose of their being and life—sanctification. To come closer to God is to become *like* God. In this way, we transcend our own being and become more human by becoming more Godlike. Being like God is in agreement with the Book of Genesis 1:26: *Let us make humankind in our image and likeness.* We are made in God's image. *God is holy. You shall be holy, for I, the Lord your God, am holy* (Lev 19:2).

When Christians speak of the imitation of God, it means imitating Christ; he is God incarnate. In his infinite love, God broke through human history and became man.

> *When the fullness of time had come, God sent His Son, born of a woman, born under the law, in order to redeem those who were under the law, so that we may receive adoption as children. And because you are children, God sent the Spirit of His Son into our hearts, crying, "Abba! Father!" So you are no longer a slave but a child, and if a child of God, then you are also an heir through Jesus Christ.* (Gal 4:4)

God took on human form, appeared on earth as Jesus Christ, in all developmental stages, so that humans could understand him. Before the world was created, Christ already existed. He was with God, and through him God made all things; not one thing in all creation was made without him. Christ was the source of life, and his life brought light to the world. His life is the light that shines through the darkness of the human condition, and the darkness can never put it out.

Christ is the perfect and living icon of the invisible God, who became visible. He is the God-man, *theanthropos*; *comely* the scripture calls him; *beautifully fashioned, full of integrity, meek and fiery, gentle and insistent.* He called himself the Son of Man, but men called him the Son of God. He healed the sick, comforted the afflicted, broke bread with the poor, and drank wine with the rich. His life on earth was marked by the miracles he performed. At his command, the blind could see, the deaf could hear, and the paralyzed could walk. He healed all kinds of sickness and cast out demons. Thousands were fed with just a few loaves of bread and a handful of fish. He walked on water, calmed a raging sea, and even raised the dead. In the stories he told and in his teachings, he emphasized that a human being should not be nourished by bread alone but must have spiritual food also. His unique message of *love* and its impact vibrated in the hearts of his followers through the centuries.

Jesus Christ is *the Way, the Truth, and the Life* (John 14:6). He speaks the words of God. He does the work of God. The person who obeys Christ follows his way and does what he does— he loves God and fulfills his will. To do this is the essence of spiritual life. Jesus has come that we may be like him and do in our own lives, by his grace, what he himself has done.

> *Very truly I say to you, the one who believes in me will also do the works that I do and, in fact, will do greater works than these, because I am going to the Father.* (John 14:12)

In all creation, including the creation of human beings, by God's power and grace the Holy Spirit is present. He is the heavenly king, the comforter, the spirit of truth, treasury and source of good things, the giver of life, who dwells among us and cleanses us from every stain of human weakness and saves our souls.

Near the end of his earthly ministry, Christ promised the presence of the Holy Spirit. He said:

If you love me, you will keep my commandments. And I will ask the Father, and he will give you another Advocate, to be with you for ever. This is the Spirit of Truth, whom the world cannot receive, because it neither sees him nor knows him. You know him, because he abides with you, and he will be with you. (John 14:15–17)

When the Spirit of truth comes, he will guide you into all the truth; for he will not speak on his own, but will speak whatever he hears, and he will declare to you the things that are to come. He will glorify me, because he will take what is Mine and declare it to you. (John 16:12–15)

Seraphim of Sarov (1759–1833), a man who seemed to live with one foot in the natural world and one foot in the supernatural, summarizes what the spiritual fathers of the early church claimed: *The very essence of life itself is the acquisition of the Holy Spirit of God.* Without the Holy Spirit, there is no true life for the human race. Further, Seraphim says:

> In spite of our sinfulness, in spite of the darkness sur-
> rounding our souls, the Grace of the Holy Spirit still
> shines in our hearts with the inextinguishable light of
> Christ…and when the sinner turns to the way of repen-
> tance, the light smooths away every trace of the sins
> committed, clothing the former sinner in the garments
> of incorruption, spun of the Grace of the Holy Spirit.

It is the presence and power of the Holy Spirit that makes our spiritual life possible. Human effort alone cannot do it. Yet, by faith and prayer we move beyond personal limitations into an awareness of the presence of God in our lives. It is our birthright to seek the kingdom within and our privilege to find it. Remember the words of Jesus: *Ask, and it shall be given you; seek and you will find; knock, and the door will be opened for you* (Matt 7:7). Consider that at the end of our days on this planet, what we earn materially stays here, but what we learn spiritually becomes our inheritance in heaven.

Thoughts to Consider:

- Your daily life, your career, your struggle to make a living, your effort to maintain your identity in our complex society consume much of your strength and time. Will you allow God to enter your daily life? Will he be with you during the many hours, thoughts, and concerns that you devote to your work and to your involvement?

- Is God a scary or remote idea? Asking God for help would not be very comforting if we thought of him as a strange power outside of ourselves—a capricious, judgmental, punitive master. God is love and his Spirit dwells in us. We are created in his image, our eternal soul, which means we are partly divine; we are sons and daughters of God.

- When we choose to believe in God and think of Jesus Christ as a living and present reality, our lives are enriched, we feel secure in his love for us. We think of what he tells us through his gospel, and we trust him to be our protector and savior; thus, life becomes more peaceful. Believing in God is a matter of choice, both yours and mine.

Step Two

Your Sacred Self

Within you exists an abundance of invisible qualities, positive and negative, which influence your daily life for better or for worse. Getting to know yourself may cause anxiety, especially if you discover negative qualities that may be stifling your success or your spiritual growth. Knowledge of self—defining, refining, and accepting who you really are—is an invaluable tool to have for your journey. As you travel, bear in mind that the more familiar you become with your self, the more rewarding will be both your immediate and future life.

Chapter 4

Self-Knowledge

Truth is within ourselves; it takes no rise from outward things, whatever you may believe. There is an inner center in us all, where truth abides in fullness; and around, wall upon wall, the gross flesh hems it in, the perfect, clear perception—which is truth.

Robert Browning

Myriad are the wonders of life, but nothing is more wonderful than a human being. Trying to understand one totally is a lifetime task. In our rapid scientific evolution, the way we view this mystery of man, in large part determines how we think, feel, act, and react toward ourselves and the world around us. In physical appearance, each of us differs from our ancestors, our parents, and the rest of humanity. As we grow, our individual character is engraved with distinctive qualities, not only by genetic predisposition, but more so by external forces. This difference of character is more pronounced as we enter our spiritual dimension, the part that is not visible. Our idiosyncrasies and perceptions are different from each other. We think, feel, act, and react differently.

How we perceive ourselves and what is the truth about ourselves are areas we need to explore in our spiritual travel. Perceptions that may be influenced by early-life programming—

by parents, teachers, or significant other adults—precipitate and dictate our choices. Our perception of who we really are may not necessarily be accurate. When people say, *I am what I am because of the way I was raised, or because of my ethnic or religious background,* or *because of things that happened to me,* they believe that they have no other choice; consequently, their self-knowledge is deficient. However, establishing the truth about ourselves, as God sees us, results in growth and self-knowledge.

One of the best ways to gain self-knowledge is to explore our current thoughts about ourselves. Upon awakening each morning, we look in the mirror; what do we think of ourselves? Truly, those thoughts precipitate *feelings* about who we are, and these feelings move on to design our daily life. In our spiritual efforts, *Who am I?* is a good question.

Each of us has an image of what we think we are or what we should be, and that image, that picture, entirely prevents us from seeing ourselves as we actually are. But when we explore ourselves with humility and without fear or preconceived notions, then we can see ourselves without distortions. People who say, *I know myself,* have already stopped learning about themselves. People who claim, *There is nothing much to learn about myself because I am just a bundle of memories, ideas, traditions, and experiences,* have also stopped learning about themselves. Learning about ourselves is always in the present. All motives, intentions, desires, pleasures, fears, inspirations, longings, hopes, sorrows, and joys are in the present. To understand anything we must live with it, we must observe it, we must know all its content, its nature, its structure, its movement, its action. To be able to know ourselves, we have to learn to live with ourselves, and this cannot be done if we are caught up with someone else's opinions, judgments, and values. If we are measuring ourselves against another whose character we happen to admire, struggling to be like that person, then we deny who we are and create an illusion.

We do not need to indulge in illusions if we wish to gain self-knowledge. We can look at the reality of Jesus Christ, the perfecter of life, and follow his teaching. Like a good sculptor, we can chisel off impurities and distortion. Then we will begin to see a new principle that we are God's people with innately wonderful and beautiful qualities. It may be hard to see, for we may not see it in ourselves. But people are real even behind their superficiality. With practice, we will find that we can look *through* them instead of just *at* them. We will salute the divinity within them and celebrate love as the one great reality in which we both live and move and have our being. This principle of love can certainly change us and the world around us. But it can only do so if we take the principle into the laboratory of our soul and roll up our sleeves. We learn to speak by speaking, we learn to walk by walking, we learn to work by working, and we can learn to love by loving. There is no other way.

Of course, when we notice our negative qualities, and we all have them, we may begin to doubt our divine gift, our ability to love. Yet, in times of great crises, when people are thrown together in the common bond of fear or concern, as in a terrorist attack, earthquake or war, illness or death, the topic of conversation often turns to how loving and mutually helpful people become. There is no logical explanation for the phenomenon other than the deeper reality. Beneath the facade of their own faulty selves, people are really good-hearted; they yearn to love and be loving. There is always enough love to go around if we are willing to turn it on by being loving. Love is one quality in our character that cannot be ignored. Learning to love enhances our knowledge of self and of God.

The axiom, *Know thyself,* is as important today as it was more than two thousand years ago when it was spoken by Socrates. Many centuries later, Shakespeare said, *To thy own self be true,* confirming the importance of self-knowledge. Clement of Alexandria, first pope of Rome, at the beginning of the second century, writes, *The greatest science for a man is to know himself, because if he knows himself, he will know God.* Later, Isaac the Syrian adds: *When a man knows himself, the knowledge of all things is available to him, for to know one's self is the fullness of the knowledge of all things.* Without knowledge of one's self, any other knowledge remains inaccurate and without purpose. When man knows himself, he recognizes the nature, the limits, and the possibilities of his existence, and he can locate himself correctly before God, his neighbor, society, and his own self.

When man attains a comprehensive knowledge of himself, he understands above all that he is not the cause of his own existence. *Who am I? Where did I come from?* become important questions. Therefore, he is led to seek the cause of his existence, which means the same thing as to seek God.

The desire to approach God and the possibility of doing so exist within our soul. How do we initiate this effort to approach God? It is possible to find the beginning within us, as Moses pointed out when he said, *The word of faith is in your heart.* We need to have faith. Remember, knowledge of self leads to knowledge of God, while faith in God results in knowledge of him, which reinforces knowledge of self. Faith and trust in God make knowledge of self possible.

Sometimes it is difficult to know who we are; yet, other voices are always available and ready to define who we are. We can reach out and find a friend with whom we can interact honestly and warmly, divulging deepest feelings, convictions, and experiences; such an interaction will give us a new dimension of ourselves but not a complete definition. A complete self-knowledge is made possible, when we solicit God's help. People with warm and receptive hearts, who believe that the Creator makes them tick, feel unconditionally accepted by God. Once they begin to feel fully accepted as they are, accepted in spite of undesirable qualities, they recognize God's love for them. Then the thought may occur, *If God really loves me, knowing who I am, I must be important in his eyes.* It is at this point that we make a transition from self-rejection to self-acceptance, which leads steadily into self-knowledge.

Isaac the Syrian (AD 339), a man of devotion and prayer, said:

> *Blessed is the man who knows his own weakness, because this knowledge becomes to him the foundation, the root, and the beginning of all goodness. For whenever a man learns and truly perceives his own weakness, at that moment he contracts his soul on every side from the laxity that dims knowledge, and develops vigilance in himself.*

In our effort to gain self-knowledge, we discover in our daily experiences a part of us yet unknown. The mystery of a human being consists of ambitions, conflicts, fantasies, feelings, and thoughts that we consciously try to process. The ancient adage, *Know thyself*, pertains to this inner exploration and development of our potential that lies in the human soul. However, in our quest for spirituality, we encounter two conflicting aspects of self: the genuine self and the false self.

The *genuine self* is what the New Testament defines as the *kingdom within*. It is the higher self, the divine part of a human being. Everything good, noble and gentle, pleasant and generous emanates from the genuine self. This self is in synchronicity with the biblical admonition described in Peter's first epistle to the Hebrews 3:8.

> Be of one mind, full of sympathy toward each other, loving one another with tender hearts and humble minds. Don't retaliate when people say unkind things about you. Instead, pay them back with a blessing. That is what God wants you to do. He will bless you for it. If you want a happy life and good days, keep your tongue from speaking evil, and keep your lips from telling lies. Turn away from evil and do good, work hard at living in peace with others.

The *false self* consists of everything negative within a person. Haunted by compulsive desires, pained by abrupt anger, frustrated by unrealistic ambitions, the person dominated by the false self is at enmity with joy. Unless repentance, forgiveness, and transformation take place, the false self's nature is in turmoil, envious, helpless, worried, critical, judgmental, unstable, in a state of perpetual dissatisfaction and unable to truly believe in God.

A vigilant heart needs to harmonize all aspects of self, filter and discipline the negative and appropriate the positive. As we diffuse pains and follies, we begin to experience inner peace and personal wisdom to pursue life and living with minimum anxiety. In this state of mind, the heart becomes aware of divine help, because it finds a certain power and assurance moving in itself. It is the heart that hears the divine whisper, telling us that this is not our ultimate home and that the things that this life offers are not totally fulfilling to our soul. The real *we*, our souls, does not value appearances, possessions, achievements, physical strength, talent, or intellect, because all these things eventually fade out and disappear. The eternal aspect of *us*, our soul beneath the surface; values the truth about who we are.

When people perceive the coming of divine help, the work of the indwelling spirit, then at once their hearts are filled with faith, and they understand, from this point on, that prayer is the refuge of help, a haven that rescues them from the tempest, a light to those who are in darkness, a shelter in time of temptation, and medication at the height of illness. Taking time out to pray helps us to connect with God and to gain better knowledge of ourselves.

Living as God wants us to live requires that you and I understand what is ours—our humanity, a composite of body and soul. We develop our body, God's gift, finding it strong, beautiful, and useful. We cultivate our mind, finding it God's greatest gift to humans when used wisely. We nurture our soul, that part which keeps our body alive while we live on this planet, and that will continue to live eternally in the life to come. Behaviorally, we are truthful—honest with ourselves and others. We are willing to take risks, to be creative, to be loving, to be competent, to change when the situation calls for it, to hold back if our sense of what is ahead seems to be dangerous. We adjust to what is new and different, keeping what is useful and discarding what is not. We think of the needs of others less fortunate and help to improve their situation. Doing these things makes us healthy, alert, sensitive, playful, loving, and productive human beings, manifesting and making available the love that God desires and the love he has for us, his creatures.

As we apply this approach in truth and not in fancy, observing this process in ourselves by participating in life and learning, then knowledge of self and knowledge of God will become realities to be cherished. Our challenge and choice will be to cease pondering vanities and remain with God by means of fervent prayer, even in time of anxiety and trepidation, lest we be deprived of the magnitude of God's presence.

Thoughts to Consider:

- Reaching within you is a calculated risk that can be rewarding. Initially you may feel afraid of what you discover about yourself. You may feel uncertain about how to change aspects of your life that are negative. Yet, from infancy to adulthood, every phase of your life went through a change. From the comfort of familiarity you moved into unfamiliar areas in spite of the discomfort. Change is an inevitable reality of life.

- Whoever you are and wherever you are, the hardest thing to transcend is the *wish* that your situation were different: that you had more time and money; that you were younger or older; that you were more talented or physically stronger; that you were single or married. Whatever your situation is, it is. Fortunately for all of us, male or female, God has given us the Holy Spirit. The power that keeps you and me alive can transform our lives.

- As you start believing in the transforming power of the Holy and life-giving Spirit, you will have an understanding of who you are, and you will have a sensation of knowing God, for he abides in you. *With God, all things are possible* the gospel reassures us. Turn inward to your spiritual self to develop your personality; examine your thoughts, behavior, and choices, and you will be in communion with the Holy Spirit.

Chapter 5

Self-Awareness

Let us make humankind in Our image and according
to Our likeness...male and female God created them.
Genesis 1:26–27

There comes a time in life when we look within ourselves
to find out who we really are. The realization and acceptance of
who we truly are enable us to provide for self-improvement and
growth. Some people look outward at the physical world and, fascinated by all its attractions, seek to surround themselves with
material possessions. Others live a conservative life, seek simplicity, are satisfied with what is available under their circumstances, and learn to adjust with the rich complexity of life.
However, for all those who desire a more rewarding and lasting
style of living, the path is unique. It starts with the simple steps
involved in learning to listen, give, pray, believe, understand,
show compassion, and appreciate what they already have. These
steps lead to the path of authentic spirituality, which is an intimate relationship with God. Attaining such a relationship is a
lifelong process. And to get started, we have to look inward to
rediscover the soul that leads and paves the way.

There is an inspiring and meaningful plot in *The Lion
King*, a Walt Disney animated and much-acclaimed motion picture. The story relates an experience of Simba, a young lion, the

son of a king and heir to his throne. Simba's Uncle Scar, the personification of evil, engineers a plot to get rid of Simba in order to steal the kingdom. The plan puts Simba in the middle of a great stampede of wild beasts; the king endangers his life and saves Simba. Uncle Scar makes sure that the king dies, and then he convinces Simba that he is responsible for his father's death.

Guilt-ridden, the young lion flees and wanders aimlessly for years, convinced by new, irresponsible companions that life should be lived carefree for the rest of his days. Simba no longer knows who he is; he abandons all anticipation of being king and leads a life of aimless irresponsibility. Meanwhile, under Uncle Scar's rule, the population suffers from hunger and despair; the devastated kingdom falls apart without caring leadership.

Simba reconnects with a baboon called Rafiki, the personification of wisdom, who knows the young lion's origins and reminds him of who he is. Rafiki leads Simba to the river and when Simba sees his reflection in the water, he says, "That's not my father. It's just my reflection."

Rafiki, possibly his conscience, says to Simba, "No, look hard. You see, he lives in you"—meaning Simba's father lives within his son.

Simba ponders the thought. Upon hearing the sound of a familiar voice, he looks upward and sees a blurred image in the sky. Hesitantly, and with a trembling voice, Simba whispers, "Father!"

"You have forgotten me," says his father.

"No, how could I?" Simba replies.

"You have forgotten who you are, and so you have forgotten me."

Simba protests, "No."

"Look inside yourself. You are more than what you have become. You must take your place in the circle of life."

"How can I go back?"—he was referring the position of being king. "I'm not who I used to be."

"Remember who you are. You are my son!"

For Simba, this is a moment of awakening and realization of who he is. Simba runs off to find and reclaim his kingdom.

Whatever the artist's intentions were in conceiving such a profound scene, it seems like a prophetic metaphor. *We have forgotten who we are.* We are sons and daughters of the most high God, and, like the young lion, instead of wandering and struggling alone in the human jungle, we need to return to the Father of all and participate in his kingdom, our kingdom.

When the disciples asked, Who is the greatest in the Kingdom of Heaven? Jesus called forth a child and said:

> *Truly, I tell you, unless you change and become like*
> *children, you will never enter the Kingdom of Heaven.*
> *Whoever becomes humble like this child is the greatest*
> *in the Kingdom of Heaven.* (Matt 18:2–4)

This powerful proclamation speaks of the condition and attitude that we need to develop. *Truly, I tell you, whoever does not receive the Kingdom of God as a little child will never enter it* (Luke 18:17). The Lord is definitive in these statements. We need to regain the faith, trust, love, innocence, and humility of little children, if we expect to be members of God's kingdom.

The Kingdom of God is within you, Jesus said (Luke 17:21). John the Baptist proclaimed, *Repent, for the Kingdom of Heaven has come near.* The return can only be effective when it is done with humility and repentance. As we fulfill God's will, we experience inner peace, beauty, and spiritual harmony.

> *Not everyone who says to me, "Lord, Lord," will enter the kingdom, but only the one who does the will of my Father in heaven.* (Matt 7:21)

Many people live with the hope and longing of bringing God's kingdom into the world as a reflection of heavenly order. *Your will be done on earth as it is in heaven,* says the Lord's Prayer. The essence of God's will is the deification, the *theosis* of people — which means that we need to be renewed according to the heavenly mode of Christ. This is not suggesting that we become Christ, but that we imitate Christ as we interact with others, as we acknowledge with respect the image of God in each of us. How we respond to another human being emotionally, physically, and verbally is of the essence. Yet, we have a model, our Lord Jesus Christ. In what manner did he encounter people? He met them with unconditional acceptance and love. When the thief acknowledged his sinful condition and said, *Lord, remember me in your Kingdom.* Christ responded, *Today you shall be with me in paradise.*

You may ask: *How can we go back and live according to his example? Especially if we feel guilty for our past mistakes or worthless in our present life?*

How did the prodigal son go back? After he had wasted all his inheritance in loose living, he thought of his father's house; full of repentance the son returned, hoping to be accepted, at least as a servant. To his surprise, his father came out to meet him, welcomed him joyfully, and gave a celebration for him. The story, in Luke's Gospel, chapter 15, speaks of our loving and forgiving Father. *His grace is abundant.*

The four gospels are not a course of sin control and punishment. They are, rather, a definition of God's unconditional love for his people. This love was manifested when the great God of the universe stooped to take on human form so that humans would understand him. God wanted to become visible, to appear in the midst of his creation, to interact with people, and there was only one thing he could do—he took on human flesh and came to us as Jesus Christ. This is the mystery of the incarnation that only the eyes of faith can visualize. Christ came into the world to teach, to heal, to restore the image of God in humans, and to reveal the truth about God.

In my mid–twenties, still in search of the answer to *Who am I?* I was fascinated with the story of Jesus and his earthly ministry. I wanted to be like him. I struggled with the belief that he was one with God. I perceived him as a great teacher, perhaps like Socrates or Plato, but greater than they were, for he possessed extraordinary powers. Then one day I came across a story, *The Hermit,* by Fr. Vincent Pottle, which I used to repeat to my children at Christmas.

I ask for the indulgence of my adult readers for using a children's story. I have a reason. All adults were once children, although most of them today do not remember much of their childhood. It is to the innocent faith of a child who is now an adult that I retell *The Hermit:*

Alone on a hilltop in a small cabin in the Midwest, this hermit lived a life of simplicity, away from worldly attractions and contemporary conveniences. He was a learned man, referred to as *the philosopher* by those who knew him. Although disenchanted by human behavior, he was kindhearted, and anyone who knocked at his door was invited in for a cup of homemade soup and a friendly chat. At nights, he always left a lighted lantern on his windowsill, a welcome sight to a passerby who might be looking for a night's lodging.

On a stormy winter night, thick snow covered the mountains and a bitter wind blew through the valleys. The hermit felt secure in his warm cabin. He hung the lantern by the window and sat by his fire, watching the leaping flames and periodically stirring a pot of boiling soup. Suddenly, he heard the sound of distant carillons. *Why are the bells ringing?* he wondered. Then it dawned on him that it was Christmas Eve.

Oh, Christmas! he smirked. *What a myth! Fancy believing that God came to earth in human form! I believe in God. But I cannot possibly believe that God would take flesh and bones and be born of a woman as a little infant, Jesus. Jesus was a good man who helped people, but I don't believe that he was God.*

He poured himself a bowl of soup and began to drink it. As he tried to dismiss the thought that God ever became a man, he heard a fluttering noise at his window. He opened his door and peered out. A flock of migrating birds was pecking at the window where the lantern was hanging. The hermit hurried back into his cabin, picked up half a loaf of bread, broke it into small pieces, and spread the crumbs on the snow where the light shone. He left his door open, hoping that the birds might sense the warmth and take refuge within. However, the birds ate the crumbs and flew off into the darkness.

Poor birds, he thought. *They will die in the storm. What a pity they could not understand there is warmth and food here. They would be safe here.* He returned to finish his soup. *I tried. What else could I have done?*

The carillons once again echoed in the cold air: *Joy to the World the Lord is here*....Then a thought surfaced in the hermit's mind. *If I could have become a bird, I could have saved those birds. Become a bird? How absurd!* he said to himself, as his whole body shook. "O God." He fell on his knees, hiding his face in his hands. "There was no other way that you could have shown your love and make us understand who you are, except by becoming a human being. You had to become human that we humans may know you."

This simple story of the hermit opened my eyes and enhanced my understanding of a profound mystery, the incarnation.

As we delve into the gospels for direction, we discover how Jesus deals with the question, *Who am I?* Jesus says that he is the Son of God (Matt 16:16–17), that he and the Father are one (John 10:30), and that the Father is the one who sent him into the world (John 5:37). He also announces that he did not come to be served, but to serve, and that he came to give his life as a ransom for many (Matt 20:28). He totally understands his purpose of being incarnate, taking human flesh, and appearing among people. His *I am* statements from the Gospel of John reveal that he claims to be the good shepherd who loves the sheep (John 10:11), the bread of life who can prevent spiritual hunger (John 6:48), and the true vine who abides in us as we abide in him (John 15:1). He also says, *I am the way, and the truth, and the life.* This statement may cause us to back away, thinking *I am not Jesus.* Of course nobody is Jesus. But through his Holy Spirit he gives us the potential to be like him, and this is the aim of a spiritual life: to make us Christlike.

In language people can understand today, Christ tells us that God is not one who lives far from us, he is not one who sees all the evil in the world and ignores it. Christ tells us that evil is not from God. God does not make evil. He hates and fights evil. He wants to eliminate evil and wipe it out totally, not just for one or two people, but for all the people of the world, not just for one day or one year, but forever.

By his exemplary life, Christ shows us that he is affected by the suffering of even one human being. He is touched by compassion and mercy at the suffering of human beings; he does not stand far off and work an occasional miracle, but he comes among us, sharing our lives with us, suffering with us every sorrow we have ever known, so that he might wipe out our suffering.

The reality of Christ is ever present. The divine becomes human so that the human may become divine. Christ's presence alone provides the hope that skepticism can never extinguish. As we connect with Christ, we feel that we are not alone, that we have God with us, not in a remote distance but very near, sharing our troubles and knowing our needs. He came to save the world, not from pain and bereavement, not even from temptation, but to save it from the power of evil in our lives, overcoming all evil by his all-powerful love.

The logos of God entered history to show humanity what human fulfillment is and to give us the means to achieve it. For each of us, the incarnation of Christ is a turning point in human destiny, a messianic deliverance from all the failures of the past. It means that there is divine assistance and power of which we can avail ourselves here and now. *For by grace you have been saved through faith, and this is not your own doing; it is the gift of God* (Eph 2:8). Our life is a gift of God, not because of who we are or what we do, but because he loves us.

Regardless of how guilty we feel about our past, God still wants us in his kingdom. We have an open invitation, which was sent through his prophets initially, and eventually through his Son, Jesus Christ. The mystery of the incarnation—God becoming man—is his ever-loving invitation. To what extent we are willing and prepared to receive the invitation is our choice.

You have forgotten who you are. The truth remains inviolate and needs to be considered. You are not a number or one of the status symbols of our time. You are eternally God's son or daughter, regardless of what has happened in your life. Regardless of your origins, however inferior, in God's eyes you are destined to be holy, and you have a purpose to serve here on earth.

There was a time when you and I did not exist. Then through our parents, in a sacred and sublime moment, the mystery of our conception and our birth took place. There will be another moment when the physical self will cease to exist. Death to our human eyes will appear as a sad and painful reality. Yet this is also a divine moment, when the soul—the invisible, changeless, eternal you—will separate from the body, to live in the presence of God forever.

Simeon, a devoutly righteous man, waited for a long time to witness the promised savior; he did not become disheartened by God's delay. When the infant Jesus was brought to the temple, as was the custom under the law, Simeon took him in his arms and praised God, saying, *Now Master, release your servant in peace…my eyes have seen your salvation* (Luke 2:25). What the Holy Spirit had revealed to him was fulfilled. The moment he saw God in human form, his life on earth felt complete. Freed from the fear of death, he was ready to return to his Creator.

When a human being meets God and comes into communion with him, he is enabled to conquer his fears, including the fear of death, and to find the meaning of life beyond earthly existence. This communion is not realized on intelligible or transcendent levels, but within the framework of everyday life, in space and time where human beings move, act, and relate with each other. How we relate with each other needs to be addressed.

It is true that you are God's creation. Do not forget who you are. Your soul knows you are eternal. When you realize that here on earth you are a son or a daughter of God, that you have a purpose, that you are destined to be a member of the heavenly kingdom, then your doubts and skepticism will evaporate. This kingdom begins right here on earth and is defined and refined as we communicate with our neighbor.

If anyone says *"I love God," and hates his brother, he is a liar; for if he does not love his brother whom he can see, how can he love God whom he cannot see?* (1 John 4:20). Love for God is seen in the love one shows for one's neighbor; and love for one's neighbor finds its fullness with the light of God's love. Church father John Chrysostom (347–407) compares the relationship that exists between love for God and love for one's neighbor with the relationship that exists between the soul and the body.

Understandably, since your birth and until this reading, you have been involved with externals, although you realize that they are always changing and shifting. One thing remains the same: your soul; from time to time you may wonder: *Am I more than what I have become?*

Truly, you are more than what you have become. By the gift of grace you are a new creation. Through the wonderful mystery of Christ's presence in your life, the image of God within you is washed clean and allowed to shine forth in greater brilliance. Chrysostom poetically describes the regenerated man and woman as "earth stars" of the day:

> *Blessed be God! Behold from the earth, stars appear, stars brighter than the ones in the sky. Stars upon earth because of Him who appeared on earth from heaven. And not only stars upon earth, but also stars in daytime—a second marvel! Stars in daytime, brighter than those of the night. The latter, of course, become hidden when the sun appears; but those stars shine forth all the more since the Son of Righteousness, Christ, has appeared. The other kind vanish when the dawn appears; but these display themselves the more since the dawn has occurred. Concerning the other kind, indeed, the Gospel says: "The stars of heaven shall fall like leaves from a vine..."; but of the human stars it says: "The righteous shall shine forth like the sun in the Kingdom of Heaven."*
>
> *Those who previously were prisoners, are now free citizens of the Kingdom. Those who formerly lived in*

the shame of their sins, now live in boldness and right-
eousness. Not only free, but also holy. Not only holy,
but also righteous. Not only righteous, but also sons
and daughters. Not only sons and daughters, but also
heirs. Not only heirs, but also brothers and sisters of
Christ. Not only brothers and sisters of Christ, but also
fellow-heirs. Not only fellow-heirs but also members.
Not only members, but the most holy. Not only the
most holy, but instruments of the Holy Spirit.

Today the struggle for survival in a materialistic world, the
search for wealth and well-being, emotional and intellectual
development, productivity and entertainment make it difficult
for us to be instruments of the Holy Spirit.

In addition to our everyday needs, we sense an immense
hunger, an inner thirst for loving communion with others, and
especially with God. To try to satisfy spiritual hunger with material acquisitions is to miss the mark; we will remain frustrated. It
is only through God's grace and guidance that we rediscover
who we are and appreciate his image in us. We need to go in the
direction pointed out by the Bible: *Trust in the Lord with all*
your heart, and lean not on your own understanding; in all your
ways acknowledge Him, and He shall direct your path (Prov
3:5–6).

In his infinite wisdom, God leads us step-by-step into the
future that he has prepared for us. In his infinite love, he reveals
to us only what is the most loving thing for us to know. God is
deeply engaged in preserving and protecting the created order.
The entire cosmos, visible and invisible, animate and inanimate,

receives life from God and exists only by virtue of his love. Each of us should follow his example so that we show similar love for his creation. He grants a fresh vision that makes the real meaning of our lives clear. No wonder that the incarnation of Christ is the central pillar of our faith and spirituality. We need to believe in Christ and to appreciate his redemptive work — creation's beauty and re-creation of our fallen humanity — with prayer and thanksgiving, knowing well its limits and its source. Our ordinary life has been touched by God, who mystically and invisibly draws all humanity and the cosmos toward its fulfillment — the *apokatastasis* — ultimate restoration. The restoring process begins the moment we connect with Christ, and it is completed in heaven.

Thoughts to Consider:

- The incarnation of Christ is a turning point in human destiny. God becomes human so that humans may become Godlike. We are all invited to share God's plan for the restoration of humanity. Passivity or neutrality toward that goal on our part is our own choice.

- A human being consists of body and spirit, and therefore our material needs must be carefully balanced with spiritual reality. Our money, time, body, sexuality, power, intelligence, science, technology, achievements, all must be used as gifts from God that glorify his Name.

- Spiritual people live in this world in the hope of Christ's final victory over the adverse powers and evil influences of this age. In the fullness of time, all life will be transformed beyond our perceptions. This is expressed in the Bible as *a new heaven and a new earth*. This transformation is not a completion of our own human plans and goals, but of God's.

Chapter 6

Self-Acceptance

Always there is a desire to accept some things and reject others. Who is making this choice and with what wisdom? Does one accept what feels good and reject what does not? Total, complete acceptance is a very real possibility.

Gerald May, MD

The inability to see the truth about one's self causes an ongoing turbulent life. Either you accept who you really are and be at peace with yourself, or you suffer slow emotional deterioration. Lack of self-acceptance blurs the vision of many situations: troubled or destructive relationships, character flaws, lingering wrong behavior, unattainable goals, financial issues, and other matters that we would rather not see clearly.

If you are unhappy or if you feel guilty about your past, remember that guilt kills. It drives people to use enormous amounts of energy in trying to hide the truths from themselves, from others, and from God. There is only one antidote for the poison of guilt: unconditional forgiveness that God provides. Forgiveness and self-acceptance allow you to have peace of mind, energy, and ability to interact with other people with a feeling of self-confidence. Accepting and forgiving yourself will make it easier for you to accept and forgive other people in your life, without an expectation that they should be different. As you realize who you are and accept yourself, then you can start making the necessary changes that you wish and move on, living a happier and more rewarding life.

The truth hurts is a familiar axiom that carries a message. Getting to know the truth, the harsh reality about who you really are, can be scary. Why? Because your identity has been defined by others—parents, peers, teachers, society, mass media—and you have accepted external opinions about who you are. But ask yourself: Can anyone really define who you are? Only you know the truth about yourself. Accept it and free yourself of irrelevant opinions. See yourself as you are. If you happen to be near a mirror, take a good look at yourself as you read this chapter and sing that old song: *I love you just the way you are.* Why not? That's the only self you have, and you might as well cherish it.

While I was in the third year of my training to become a psychologist, I woke up one day, an unusual dream still in my head. The setting was a Los Angeles cathedral in California, a church in which I had served as a priest for ten years. I dreamed that I had invited my congregation to attend my funeral. I stood behind a casket that was surrounded by flowers, and as the music faded out I spoke my own eulogy: "Beloved friends, I bring you here today to tell you the truth about myself, because I know that when I die my colleagues and friends will most likely praise and even exaggerate my virtues. They will not say anything negative about me, lest they hurt anyone's feelings. So I bring you here today that you may hear from my own lips the truth about me."

At that moment the congregation burst out with noisy comments: *The truth...the truth...Oh, he's probably going to confess his sins.*

Upon awakening, I felt rather disturbed. Although the dream had ended, my curiosity increased by the moment. Two hours later, I found myself at Dr. Herbert Holt's office in New York City, seeking an analysis of my dream. The aging yet ageless therapist looked at me with a smile and said, "Peter…Peter, you are too naive. You wanted to tell your people the truth about yourself? What is truth? Do you know the truth about yourself— who you really are?"

"I think I do."

"If you do, why didn't you tell the gathering?"

"I woke up," I said emphatically.

"Of course. You could not endure hearing yourself telling the truth." Noticing the grimace of disbelief on my face, he said, "We humans have a problem accepting the reality about who we are. We would rather be our fantasies, or we would rather hear others praising us so that we may be comforted."

In the days that followed, I pondered Dr. Holt's interpretation of my dream. I reexamined my life, and I compared my behavior with the expectations of the Ten Commandments and with certain principles of my Christian faith. I realized that my dream had a message. I was not really who I thought I was. Dr. Holt was right. Had I continued with my eulogy, telling my audience the whole truth about myself—injustices, wrongs, violations, sins, and all kinds of unwitting errors—I would probably have run away to avoid the embarrassment.

What happens when we run away? Geography does not change our status; we take ourselves with us wherever we go. A positive approach is to look within and determine what we need

to do and what direction to take. In his poignant poem, Edward
Sandford Martin presents us with something to think about.

> *Within my earthly temple there's a crowd,*
>> *There's one of us that's humble; one that's proud.*
> *There's one that's broken-hearted for his sins,*
>> *And he who, unrepentant, sits and grins.*
> *There's one who loves his neighbor as himself,*
>> *And one who cares for naught but fame and pelf.*
> *From much corroding care would I be free*
>> *If once I could determine which is Me.*

At some point in your life, you need to determine which is
you, which is *me*. After years of self-scrutiny and self-repair, I
came to realize which was me and what I had to do to face the
truth about myself. For example, I had to put in perspective the
wrongs and the injustices done to me, and I wasted no more time
thinking of the "evildoers" in my life. It was not easy, but to
maintain emotional, mental, and spiritual health, I had to let go
of the past. And to reinforce the present me, it was imperative to
also forgive myself. If God's forgiveness is abundantly available to
each of us, it was time to forgive myself for whatever wrong I had
done and to be sensitive enough not to repeat it.

I believe there are three kinds of truth: how we perceive
ourselves; how we are perceived by others, which keeps us comfortable as we interact with them; and what God thinks of us.
One sure way to redefine and accept ourselves is to compare and
combine God's guidance for us with our thoughts about ourselves. Ultimately, how you define yourself and how you accept

yourself is a personal choice that you may consider. What I have applied in my life that seemed to work for my self-acceptance was to make an honest effort to correct parts of my life that could be corrected and leave other parts that could not be corrected in God's loving care and forgiveness.

Whether you are a man or woman, young or old, to enhance and fortify the process of self-acceptance, you may consider the points made by *The Man in the Glass*, a familiar poem by an anonymous author.

When you get what you want in your struggle for self
And the world makes you king for a day,
Just go to a mirror and look at yourself
And see what that man has to say.
For it isn't your father or mother or spouse
Whose judgment upon you must pass;
The fellow whose verdict counts most in your life
Is the one staring back from the glass.

Some people may think you a straight-shootin' chum
And call you a wonderful guy,
But the man in the glass says you're only a bum
If you can't look him straight in the eye.
He's the fellow to please, never mind all the rest,
For he's with you clear up to the end.
And you've passed your most dangerous test
If the man in the glass is your friend.
You may fool the whole world down the pathway of life,
And get pats on your back as you pass.

But your final reward will be heartaches and tears
If you've cheated the man in the glass.

There may be no satisfactory answer to the awesome mystery of the human face that scrutinizes itself in the mirror. The ever-flowing facets of one's personality move on at such a miraculous pace that we lack power to capture a congruent definition. If you have difficulty in defining and accepting who you are, a physical and spiritual entity, then your world becomes a dilemma: Who am I? Why was I born? What am I doing here? Is there a life after death? What is expected of me? What can I expect of others?

An unexamined life is not worth living is an axiom attributed to Socrates the Greek philosopher. As a contemporary Greek-American, not a philosopher, I would like to add a clause to this thought: *An overexamined life can be a menacing hell.* I don't mean to be aloof or irreverent to my ancestor's dictum, but please follow me briefly.

Let's watch the evening news, the demonic demonstration of tragedy, which actually happened to our nation on September 11, 2001. Then let's hear the overemphasized description of imminent terrorism predicting what "might happen" to us. "Terror Alert" in red letters flashes on the screen of every television set. The overwhelming dose of danger of biochemical weapons haunts our human existence. You and I, potential victims of such frenzy, fear, anxiety, insecurity, and death, shrink from the very thought.

In view of this colossal confusion of conflicts, attacks, violence, war, what can we do to create a less stressful and more viable life? There is no guide, no teacher, no authority to relieve

us from this anguish. Many people have become deeply disillu-
sioned, for they find no fulfillment in a world overfilled with self-
improvement methods. Others concern themselves with
methods of self-enrichment, techniques for personal growth, and
they, too, find no inner peace.

As a nation and as a culture, we have learned so much that
we wonder what value there is in more knowledge. Some hard-
working individuals who have become affluent now wonder
what purpose is served in having power, luxury, and wealth.
Hearing or reading about the private or not so private lives of the
rich and famous, one tends to analyze every aspect of life, hopes
and impulses, intentions and goals, fears and faiths.

Quo Vadis?—Where are you going? Issues and questions
come from the voice within. As troublesome as these questions
may be, it is possible that they mark the path to a spiritual life—
a spiritual life that is not attained in heaven; a spiritual life that
starts here on earth, as you are holding this book. At this
moment, there is only you and me and our faith in a loving God
who will protect us from all impending fears. Blaming the bar-
baric people and their power-thirsty leaders, and investing more
time in how we could destroy them, becomes a hideous, unseen
warfare that saps our energy and submerges us to more despair.

This is the world we live in, a place infiltrated by evil and
permeated by fear. You and I did not make it this way; we wish
for peace and security. Once we accept the realities of life, we
realize that peace and happiness are a result of our mode of
being in this world. Ultimately, we have to accept our own reality, which is a composite of positive and negative qualities. As we
understand our life, our frustrations, our infantile need to con-

trol others, our inability to accept and love, we also understand that nobody on earth is going to rescue us. Only the Creator and Sustainer of the Universe can do that, and it is up to you and me to trust his everlasting and unconditional love.

As you embrace the idea that God loves you unconditionally, learn to practice unconditional acceptance. Reduce your expectations of other people; ask nothing of anyone. Then reach within your soul where there is unconditional acceptance. This requires that you empty your mind of judgments. Such an act might appear to be an impossible task, but before rejecting it, continue the process of acceptance for one week and see if you don't soon experience a new kind of serenity. Do not underestimate the power of your soul, that invisible spirit which is a part of your being. *The kingdom of heaven is within you* is not merely a poetic verse, it is a reality. God will work with you because he brought you into this world for a purpose. See that truth in all of the people you encounter. Imagine yourself as just a soul interacting with other souls. Try to treat others as God's children. In every one, his spirit abides, and he cares for each one as he cares for you.

Suspend your negative thoughts for one or two days. You don't need to prove the other person wrong or to prove yourself right. When you look toward God for help, you notice that in his eyes we are equals. Each person is entitled to have his or her point of view. If you want to see the spiritual dimension in your life, simply let go of your need to make anyone else wrong for a few days. Detach yourself for a brief period from the behavior of controlling others through your position of authority, physical appearance, age, size, education, wealth, or anything external to yourself.

Avoid dictating to those who are smaller, younger, or less educated. We are all at different stages on the spiritual path of life, but none of us is "better" than anyone else. We are just different.

Thoughts to Consider:

- A woman who gives birth to a child automatically offers love and acceptance. She knows within her heart what to do, what to give to her infant without expectations. She is willing to accept the worst and responds with acceptance and love. Can you think of this model and accept yourself and others without expectations?

- Acceptance does not imply endorsement of inappropriate or wrong behavior. It simply refers to a state of mind that allows you to be peaceful and know the difference between things you can help improve and things that are the way they are. As the Serenity Prayer claims: *God, grant me the serenity to accept the things I cannot change, the courage to change the things that I can, and the wisdom to know the difference.*

- Self-acceptance is a state of mind. It does not come from living up to some society-designated measure of performance. It does not come by comparing yourself with others. It is attainable when you live with the knowledge that you are operating at your own peak performance, using with gratitude the gifts and abilities God gave you to their full intended extent.

Body, Not the Total Self

Greater than your persona, during your present life on this planet Earth, is your inner self, your soul. This everlasting part of your being, which God gave you at birth, will continue to live on beyond death. Your soul, the spiritual dimension of your physical self, is God's gift to humans, the mystery that keeps you alive. Gleaning from the inspiration of philosophical thought and scriptural sources, you can arrive at some personal awareness of your soul and its significance. This is a promising challenge.

Chapter 7

Soul—Your Immortal Self

*The soul forms the body, yet it is itself without body
and therefore it cannot be located in an organ. Because
of its incorporeality, the soul's beauty is harder to see.
The soul is concerned with goodness and beauty, with
justice and courage, with friendship and loyalty.*

James Hillman

When we ask, *What is the soul?* it is like asking, *What is
God?* Does anyone know? To attain any assured knowledge
about the soul is one of the most difficult things in the world.
Science, by engaging the mind, logic, and reason, explores and
defines whatever is tangible with sufficient accuracy. However,
unseen realities—God, angels, the soul, the spirit—require faith,
assisted by religious and philosophical thought. Our aim to grasp
and understand, even partially, the essence and properties of the
soul requires spiritual resources. It can only be done in the
human heart, not in a scientific laboratory. Progressive knowledge about the soul contributes to our understanding of ourselves, God, and the world around us.

Since the beginning of time, when human beings wondered about life and death, they gradually became aware of
another dimension of their existence. Beyond their physical
being, which changed and suffered variations, they perceived an

internal strength, a life force that activated their body, which caused thoughts such as, *If you and I can build a shelter to house our bodies, there must be a master builder who created this Earth and the whole universe.* We call this part of our human being the soul. The soul searches for the Creator beyond the physical world.

The soul is the unseen part of our body that makes it possible for us to know that we are God's creations. Just as God rules and animates the world, so does the soul give life and activates the body. Because the soul is a spiritual reality, it does not die. From ancient times to the present day, philosophers, sages, and wise teachers have always believed that although the physical self ages and dies, the soul lives on.

Plato (428–348 BC), in Phaedo's dialogue, says:

> *The soul is invisible, pure and noble, and on her way to the good and wise God. That soul departs to the invisible world—to the divine and immortal. Upon arriving, she lives in bliss and is released from the error and folly of men, their fears and wild passions and all other human ills, and forever dwells in company of gods.*

The question of the immortality of the soul was the principal subject of Plato's speculations. He believed that upon death, the soul leaves the body and enters a new world, invisible to our physical eyes, and lives forever in the presence of God.

Among the neo-Platonists the dualism of body and soul is distinct. Spirit is essentially good, and matter is essentially evil. Therefore, the body is the "prison," the "tomb," or even the "hell" of the soul—implying that the body is the seat of all sin. Implicit here is the thought that as the soul leaves the body, it liberates itself.

The followers of Pythagoras (580–500 BC) taught that the soul was a harmony, its essence consisting of those perfect mathematical ratios that are the laws of the universe and the music of the heavenly spheres.

Pythagoras required his followers to lead a harmonious life by practicing virtues: loyalty, resistance to temptations, truthfulness, generosity, honesty, hospitality, *whatever is good and beautiful*. Men and women who attended his school in southern Italy were required to practice these spiritual disciplines through self-examination. Pythagoras commanded:

> *Do not go to sleep before you examine and question three times your deeds of the day: "What have I trespassed? What good deed have I done? What should I have done but omitted doing?" When you realize that you have done wrong things, reprimand yourself, and if you have done good deeds, rejoice. This you must practice, this you must study, this must be your daily course, because this will put you on the path to divine virtue.*

Defined by the Pythagorean school, virtue is order, harmony, and health of the soul. Education should aim at the cultivation and establishment of virtue.

The Stoics taught that all existence was material, and they described the soul as a breath pervading the body. They called it divine—in Greek, *apospasma tou theou*, that is, a particle of God composed of the most refined and ethereal matter, whose seat is the heart, the center of the cognitive and emotional life.

In the Book of Genesis, we learn that God forms Adam's body and then he breathes into it and creates the soul. The in-breathing of God is the energy of the Holy Spirit. It is this energy that created the soul. The soul cannot be examined apart from its Creator. In Hebrew, three terms are used for the soul: *nephesh*, referring to the animal and vegetative nature, *nuah* referring to the ethical principle, and *shesamah*, referring to the purely spiritual intelligence. The Old Testament asserts or implies the distinct reality of the soul. In later Jewish thought, Philo of Alexandria teaches with conviction about the divine origin of the soul. But Christianity brings all definitions of the soul to full focus. Tertullian, a Christian of the early church, speaks eloquently of the failure of all philosophies to elucidate the nature of the soul. He points out that only Christ can teach humankind the truth on such a subject. Truly, Christ's teachings do center around the spiritual side of human nature:

> *You shall love the Lord your God with all your heart, and with all your soul and with all your mind. This is the greatest and the first commandment....What shall be the benefit to a man who gains the whole world and loses his soul? What could he give in exchange of his soul?....Be not afraid of those that would kill your body...but rather fear those who can destroy both soul and body.*

St. Paul consistently appropriates *psyche*—the soul—for the natural life. For the supernatural or spiritual life, he uses the term *pneuma*—spirit—which is the Holy Spirit, dwelling and operating in the human heart.

Philosophical and religious thought throughout written history indicates our human realization that we are not simply flesh, bones, and blood. We consist of a physical body and an inner force that animates the body. In most religions, the inner force is known as the *soul*. Both body and soul coexist simultaneously without any confusion. We are aware that we are more than mere physical entities. There is another part in us that is unseen, yet ever present in our lives.

The human soul is multifaceted. It may be considered as trinitarian in nature: the Greek words *nous*, *logos*, and *pneuma* have their own special connotation—*nous* is the thinking part and core of human existence; the *logos* is the expression of thought and perception of the *nous*; and *pneuma*, the spirit, is the vivifying force of human life.

Although the soul abides in the body, it is not located in only one part of the body. There is no functional part of the body in which the soul is not wholly present. In all religions, God acts in nature and governs the universe; in like manner, the soul moves and activates each member of the body to perform its function. It fills the entire body, giving it life. Simply put, the soul is not enclosed by the body, but it occupies the body to which it is attached. The soul is not held by the body, but it is the soul that contains the body and gives it life.

In a time of prayer or meditation, as we get deeper into our self, we become more aware of the unseen attributes that are properties of our soul:

1. **The conscience** is an inner voice that guides us through life's choices and decisions. It is a part of our being that praises what is good and beneficial and judges or even reprimands what is evil and destructive. It is our innate inward call to become part of the body of Christ. The perfection of conscience is *agape* — love.

2. **The mind,** *nous* — that is, *the highest human faculty* — is the ability to think and reason, which precipitates emotions, actions, movements, and survival skills. It is a part of our being that conceives ideas and pursues or avoids their fulfillment. When it is purified, the mind perceives God and his creation.

3. **The free will** is a human prerogative to make choices, to discern good and evil. As we harmonize conscience, mind, and heart, we can decide with greater confidence what action is proper. We have the freedom to pursue good or evil, to create or to destroy, to live a good life or a destructive life, to love and forgive or to hate. Such discernment results in a life of wisdom, which is the perfection of know-how in being a responsible member of society and, eventually, of God's kingdom.

4. **The heart** is the center of the human psychosomatic constitution. There is an unconfused union between soul and body. The center of this union is called heart. Therefore, the heart is not only the physical organ that pumps blood through our body, but it is the source of all emotions; it has the abundant capacity for spiritual feelings such as compas-

sion, faith, hope, and love. This capacity indicates that we are not only physical entities; we are also spiritual beings.

5. **The soul's faculty** is expressed in universal yearning for God. Nothing in the created world is capable of satisfying the soul. Created by God, the soul seeks and wants to live in communion with God. Until the soul has attained this, it cannot find peace. How much better it would be, day by day, to move our life in the direction of God in which the soul, light as a feather, fluid as water, innocent as a child, responds to every movement of God's grace.

Accepting the concept of such an unexplored potential, relating to God, intrinsic qualities that are good in us, can mean the difference between success and failure, love and hate, happiness and unhappiness.

Like the conductor of an orchestra, the soul harmonizes our patterns and inner qualities to give us a fuller sense of who we are and a better appreciation of our purpose on this planet. This activity of the soul releases the divine energy within, restores our daily life, and brings us closer to our Creator. Although invisible to the human eye, our soul is the divine part of our humanity, which needs to be cared for and nurtured.

Thoughts to Consider:

- *Become partakers of the divine nature, your soul. For this very reason, make every effort to supplement your faith with virtue, and virtue with knowledge.* (Apostle Peter)

- *Get deeper into yourself; explore your soul, the spiritual part of you, and learn from your inner self what you must do.* (An Ancient Adage)

- *The ladder that leads to the Kingdom of Heaven is hidden within you, and it is found in your own soul. Dive into your self, and in your soul you will discover the rungs by which to ascend.* (St. Isaac the Syrian)

Chapter 8

The Voice of Your Soul

*Paying attention to our external life—what our body
looks like, what others think of us, how much money
we are making, how we may impress others—leaves
the soul unattended. External aspects of life create an
emptiness within, a sense of shallowness. The less significance we give our thoughts, the easier it will be to
connect with our soul. As we keep nourishing the soul,
we move on to an entirely different level of life.*

Richard Carlson, PhD

My soul has a voice? Yes! Deep down in your heart, you
know what is a good thing to do, a bad thing to avoid, and
which is the right direction to take. The voice of the soul may
be silent, but its message is of great importance in your life.
Like a wise and gentle teacher, this inner voice invites you to
follow as it leads you toward a sense of purpose and meaning.
To become aware of this inner compass, for a precious moment
sit in a quiet place, close your eyes, breathe in deeply, empty
your mind of idle thoughts and concentrate on that part of your
being that is invisible to the human eye. As you explore your
inner territory, remain still and wait until you begin to notice a
feeling of tranquility. This is the dawn of a new horizon, a ray
of hope and joy.

Many people feel it is a sign of weakness or ignorance when they realize that they do not understand something. Reading about spiritual issues—faith, God, soul, spirituality—might evoke insecure thoughts in your mind, even some doubts about their existence. Do not be alarmed; it is matter of strength, an opportunity to learn and experience something different. When a room is dark, what do you do? Your first reaction is to reach for a light switch or light a candle. When the room is illumined, you feel safe, for you do not have to grope your way around in the darkness. Psalm 119: 130 offers us a helping hand, leading us to focus on God when in doubt: *The unfolding of Your words gives light; it gives understanding to the simple.* This is a viable option.

Steven, a college graduate with a master's degree in sociology and a PhD candidate, admitted to his family that he could no longer believe in God. His skepticism reached the point of atheism. His parents, devoted to their Christian faith, were devastated. "We spent all that money to turn our son into an atheist," his father stated with sadness.

Hearing the comment, Steven's grandfather smiled and said, "Your son gained a lot of knowledge; now he may need to mature." The following day, the old man was pruning a pine tree in his backyard. Steven approached his grandfather to inquire about the drastic cutting.

"You know, trees like humans need to let go of the excess growth," said his grandfather.

"I don't understand what you mean," said Steven.

"There are many things that I don't understand, myself, such as cellular phones, e-mail, and television, but there is one thing that I totally understand. There is a God in charge of the whole world. He even causes this tree to grow."

"Where is God, Grandpa? I don't see him." Steven giggled.

"Come. I'll show you where he is."

Steven, with a grimace of doubt, followed his grandfather. It was noontime and the sun was bright and hot.

"Look up there, keep your eyes on the sun," the grandfather said.

Steven looked up for a while and then turned his face away. "Keep looking straight at the sun," the grandfather insisted.

Steven covered his face. "My eyes are hurting; I can't do it."

"Well, young man, if you cannot see the sun, how do you expect to see the one who created the sun?"

"Grandpa, you're a wise man."

"I don't have much education, but I believe in the miracle of creation. Look around you, Steven. A tree, a rose, a daisy, a blade of grass—each form has its own life and expression, each tree its own shape, each flower its own fragrance, a miracle that only God can perform."

Steven had worked himself to exhaustion to earn his master's degree and he planned to work just as diligently on a doctorate. At the same time, eager to get a job, he had sent out résumés and scheduled interviews, but he did not get any job offers. He worked himself into a state of anxiety and frustration. How could he think of God's presence in his life when he doubted his own strengths? Truly, the complex problems of our times tempt us to pessimism and bring us moral paralysis. The world shouts at us everyday: *Go this way! Come over here! Go with the flow!* Billboards line our landscape, luring us with larger-than-life enticements. Clever and colorful advertisements inundate our mail. Television, radio, movies, even our computers now clamor at higher and higher decibels to tell us where to turn, what to buy, what to think! Confusion and saturation lead to doubt and pessimism. What a waste of time!

Our spirit within, however, rarely shouts directives at us, and it has its own good reason. The soul's voice refuses to compete for our attention with all the other voices that pound in our eardrums. Often, when our soul speaks, it whispers so softly that we miss the message if we are not focused on it. That is why spending a little time in prayer each day is important. We have to believe that we can make a difference. Acting on this belief, we become people of the spirit. Then we can move forward in faith that God is there and he cares.

God is not in heaven fretting that our choices mess up his plans for us. He is in control of our lives and the lives of those we love, even when we cannot see his hand or hear his voice as clearly as we wish. Sometimes we lack the confidence to take this important step, particularly when, having done all we can do to make our lives better, we still are not certain which direction to take. We still feel immobilized for fear of making a mistake. What can we do with those lingering doubts that leave us in a haze?

Doubts do not necessarily mean that you are not a spiritual person. In spite of your fears, you can still move ahead because your confidence is based not on your physical body alone but on your spiritual self, your soul. *Be of good cheer*, Jesus tells us. So take courage! Turn your crossroad into a faith-road, and let the journey begin. Next time you come up against an area of doubt or skepticism, admit to yourself that you have a hard time accepting certain matters that are not tangible. Spiritual realities are difficult to perceive and resolve with rational thinking alone. However, faith and honesty provide opportunities to learn; they also remove the strain of defensive egotism, prevent and clarify inner conflict, and bring about peace of mind.

Each day, you meet your physical needs—eating, resting, and sleeping at regular intervals. Think of making time for spiritual renewal. If we neglect our bodies, they become weak and break down. If we neglect our spiritual needs, we become emotionally confused, and conflicts disturb our daily life. When the vision becomes blurred, it is time to close our eyes and reflect by going deeper into ourselves and seeking the power that nurtures life.

To be able to identify with this powerful essence of your life, I suggest that you choose a time during the day when you feel relaxed and unpressured. Sit quietly in a comfortable chair and close your eyes. Slowly become aware of your breathing and follow the stream of breath entering though your nose and going out of your body through your mouth. Imagine your whole body rising and falling with the flow of your breath. After a couple of minutes, as your muscles relax, visualize your body permeated by a warm current. You may even feel a sudden shiver in your spine. Try this exercise regularly for a week or two and you will notice an inner force vivifying your life. This is your soul in action. Do not ignore its presence.

What Thomas Moore calls "psychological modernism" is an area of concern for people who truly care about their lives. It is of benefit to observe and avoid the uncritical acceptance of the lifestyle dictated by clever advertising. We have to be careful about conforming to contemporary values, thinking that we live in a modern world. Everything available to us is not necessarily of benefit to our well-being. We may obsessively collect things, anxiously try to catch up with scientific progress, and attach ourselves to electronic media and material gadgets; all these can become emotional crutches, an illusion of security in an insecure world. We cannot find security outside ourselves, and certainly not behind walls of clutter. We find security by looking within our spiritual essence and living with integrity.

I recall my teenage years, living in a Greek village occupied by Nazis during World War II. Food was scarce, and to cook, I had to chop wood for the fireplace. My family and I did without electricity and running water. We lit oil lanterns in the evening. From the community well, I drew water for drinking and washing. Doctors and drugstores were not available, so when I fell sick, I faced illness with homemade remedies and my grandmother's prayers. Imagine advising a patient today to drink herbal tea and have prayers offered. Yet such experiences make a person simple, and how difficult it is to be simple when you live in a materialistic world! Seeking simplicity in a world of wealth and material affluence is a challenge. Yet scaling down and becoming more conscious of how we appropriate our material possessions create inner joy and peace for people and their immediate environment.

In our daily lives, we could seek simplicity by bearing in mind that there are other people in this world whose boundaries need respect and protection. Think of yourself leaving your home in the morning to go to work. Hurriedly, you get into your car and move on to beat the traffic. Suddenly, you think of something important, and while you are on the highway with speeding cars on either side, you pull out your cellular phone to make a call. Dangerous? Yes! I have seen many car accidents involving drivers who steer with one hand and hold the phone in the other. If the call is that important, why not pull over to the side, stop the car, and make the call? Not only would you be able to focus and make clear sense to the other party, but you would be safeguarding your life and the lives of others. As you become aware of your thoughts, your actions will have more rewarding consequences.

Many people start the day with meditation, prayer, and exercise. Others have a daily ritual of taking a walk early in the morning or in the evening after work to unwind.

Whichever ritual nurtures your life, it is important that you do it consistently. It does require some degree of discipline, but once you transcend the resistance or excuses, you will be surprised at the benefit you will reap.

Pat, my lovng wife, begins each day with prayer, reading verses from the Bible, and taking a mile walk on the treadmill. Before sunrise, she says her prayer in a small sanctuary that, over the years, she has designed. If time permits, she gets on the treadmill in the morning; otherwise she does her walking in the evening. Then, with a cup of herbal tea in one hand and the Bible in the other, she sits by the deck and reads. Watching the sunrise and the changing sky, listening to the birds chirping, and admiring the busy squirrels and rabbits running through the backyard, she smiles, sensing the awakening of life. It is time for her to go to work.

My day begins a little differently. Two things are imperative to start my day: prayer and exercise. As I look through the window, I whisper a few words of gratitude, *Thank You, Lord, for another day.* Then I pick up a certain book that I have started and I read for fifteen minutes. As I close my book, I think of the clients who are scheduled for the day, and I ponder their concerns about life. I try to develop a direction for each of them so their session with me will be productive. After a light breakfast, I make a list of three tasks that need to be done. One of them may be totally personal—doing something for fun. Either I meet a friend for lunch, or I go to the YMCA for a swim. The other two tasks are work-oriented. Sometimes, when there is an emergency, my routine is changed or totally skipped.

I do not presume that each reader of this book has to follow the above ritual. What works well with one person may not be as effective with another. However, this small daily experience paves the way toward my personal spirituality. It is close to home and is especially nourishing to my soul. I am fully aware that my ritual does not cover the whole concept of spirituality. There is a lot more that I do in my pursuit of a sound spiritual life. Yet, without this simple daily ritual, religion can become far removed from my human condition; it can even be irrelevant. People can be extremely religious in that they attend church regularly, give large donations, follow the rules, and yet be subject to materialism and profess values in everyday life that are totally secular.

Think of the following truism: There is one inescapable reality. You and I live and shape our lives the way we choose. You are the authority of your life, not the absolute authority—that belongs to God. You design your life according to your emerging conscious or unconscious needs. Regardless of what others think or say, when you manage to develop a personal ritual and follow it consistently, you are going to notice a smooth and pleasant change in your personal life and in the life of those who live with you.

Thoughts to Consider:

- Sit in a quiet, comfortable place where external sounds will not disturb you. Gently place your hand over your heart and feel the regular beat. You are alive! Ask: "Who or what causes my heart to beat?"

- Ask a second question; it is of equal importance: "How can I better hear the voice of the one who keeps my heart beating? How can I sharpen my hearing so that I can distinguish my own soul's voice from the voices of others?" Well-meaning friends will comfort you by offering advice, which may give you some relief. However, when you are alone in quietness, your soul's voice will speak to you about issues that you may have to face. Stay calm and listen.

- Imagine hearing the voice of your soul. What is it saying to you about your life, family, friends, neighbors, or workplace? Could this inner voice appreciate who you are and what you have? Devote more time to personal renewal. Be kind and generous. Share more of your time and energy with others who need your presence.

Chapter 9

Caring for Your Soul

Soul-caring is a life-time effort, intuition, knowledge, skill and courage. All of us yearn excessively for entertainment, power, intimacy, sexual fulfillment, and material things. We think we can find these things if we discover the right relationship or job, the right church or therapy. But whatever we find, does it satisfy the soul?

Thomas Moore

Deep inside you, unknown to your five senses, is an innermost core of being, an unchangeable spirit that animates, shapes, and forms your personality. Unlike the engine of your car, it functions without your consent to maintain action, life, harmony, and movement. This being, known as spirit or soul, is your essential state—it is who you really are.

This most precious part of your existence that separates you from the animal kingdom resides in your body. As your body needs proper care, so your soul also requires sensitive care. When your soul is well cared for, you will always have your best friend and companion within you. In your quest for happiness and peace, caring for the soul becomes an imperative task. When you observe how the soul manifests itself and how it operates, you discover ways to nurture it.

People whose souls are troubled resort to psychiatry and psychotherapy. Truly, each of the disciplines has its individual importance, and in time of need each makes a significant contribution to health and life. Each helps to relieve people from anxiety and stress, from negative moods and emotions; each reveals bad life choices and unhealthy habits, and, without judgment, each points out how human mistakes and failures provide the best lessons in life.

Realizing that most emotional and some physical ailments are caused by a suffering soul, the medical community has shown an increasing interest in the spiritual life of its patients. It is evident that people who believe in God and pray frequently have a positive attitude, a sense of well-being, and they seem to recover rapidly from setbacks.

Professionals acknowledge that many of the major diseases—heart problems, cancer, lung ailments, accident injuries, and alcoholism—are related in part to our neglect of our soul and to our collective lifestyle. The human being is a psychosomatic unity. We should not separate body and soul, for when we do, our physical, spiritual, and emotional health is threatened. When a garden is neglected weeds grow, the soil dries up, and nothing is produced. A neglected soul is an ailing soul, and its influence can permeate our personality and make daily life difficult.

Recent years have brought an intense interest in emotional health and spirituality. Churches, temples, and faith communities exert concerted efforts to provide programs, retreats, and workshops to nurture the soul. Yet, whatever good and spiritually beneficial means they make available, external cares and concerns of life defuse these offerings and render them impotent.

The increasing need to have a successful life, to make more money, to have a better home with all of the latest conveniences, to impress others and be accepted by everyone, does not leave much room to see the real and lasting part of you, your soul.

Marilyn, an attractive brunette, reached the top of the ladder of success by the age of thirty-four. She fulfilled the American dream—a loving husband, a substantial income, a beautiful home, two children, and a nanny—a life that was envied by her neighbors and peers. But something seemed to be missing in her life, making her unhappy. In the early years of her marriage, she was devoted to her faith and attended church regularly. When children entered her life and work demanded more of her time, she gradually gave up her church activities. She was a busy working mom. She experienced bouts of depression and moodiness; she had a hard time understanding herself. Minor matters irritated her and made her angry; when a conflict occurred between her and work or within a relationship, she became explosive.

Marilyn paid meticulous attention to details, and she was precise in everything she did, but to her nothing seemed good enough. Her home, where every item was perfectly arranged, could be better. *Why can't I be like Martha Stewart?* When her employer complimented her on her work, she beamed at the time, but the satisfaction did not last long. *I should do better*, she would say to herself. *Why didn't things turn out the way I want them: perfect?*

She was a perfectionist, and her passion for perfection left no room for compassion for others. As a result, she alienated herself from people. Her schedule was crammed with commitments. Eventually she distanced herself from her family. She rarely spent time with her husband, who eventually resented her enthusiasm over her passion. One evening he said, "Marilyn, I can't take this pressure much longer. You are trying to do too much. You freak out when things don't turn out the way you planned. Our children are feeling your tension. I feel frustrated because nothing that I do or suggest seems to please you." It seemed evident that if children had not been involved, her husband would have walked out of the marriage.

When Marilyn came to my office, she admitted that she was a very unhappy person. "I expect everyone in my life to see things my way."

"That must give you some satisfaction," I said.

"Yes! I can't stand mediocrity. When I do something, it has to be perfect."

I asked, "What do you find difficult about perfection?"

"It makes me vulnerable. I would like to be successful, but I am driving myself and my family crazy."

"How do you know when your perfectionism is too much?" I asked, still trying to speak for her soul's need for perfection.

"When I don't feel good about myself. I feel very irritable. Even little things bother me."

As a psychotherapist, I could probe deeper into her past, search for early traumas, childhood experiences, and seek to trace the origins of Marilyn's problem. Conceivably, she could have experienced conditional acceptance at home. She was the oldest of three sisters. Her own parents probably expected her to perform above and beyond all standards. Most likely she cooperated with this dictum by excessive striving and developing an overserious preoccupation with achievement in order to gain approval. She lived with a constant feeling of unworthiness, because she did not think she could meet her parent's expectations.

Continuing with my original approach, I said, "I wonder if you could find a way to be a perfectionist without feeling bad about it? After all, people receive a great deal of praise and admiration when they strive for perfection."

In the following session, Marilyn admitted that she had always assumed that spontaneity was desirable and perfection was unattainable. Our dialogue revealed that she was enthusiastic about spontaneity, and she did not enjoy the pursuit of perfection.

The more she pushed for adequacy, the less adequate she felt. Her new direction to seek spontaneity, even if her accomplishments were less perfect, might be a way of avoiding and repressing the strong need in her to be perfect. Being that she was a Christian, I offered what I thought was God's view of human perfection. I did not approach the subject in a preaching manner for that might have bothered her. A homeopathic move, going with the symptom that she presented rather than against it, was to indicate how to be perfect in a manner that was satisfying. In a way, I was proposing the possibility of self-acceptance.

"Don't you want to live and love life, appreciate what you have accomplished thus far, enjoy your kids, and cherish the presence of your mate and children to the point that you couldn't live without them?"

"Of course," she said. "That sounds like perfection."

"Well, like anything else in life, you can't have it without its shadows: There is always the sense of not enough, the need to be

in control, the inability to please everybody, the desire to compete and surpass all others."

Marilyn's soul had the need to be perfect. She had to realize that only God is perfect. When Jesus invites people to be perfect—*Be as perfect, as my Father in Heaven is perfect*—the call is
to continue to grow and mature. It does not mean to compare or
to compete yourself with God. It does not mean never making an
error or a mistake. It means looking at yourself objectively,
accepting and recognizing your strengths and talents, as well as
areas of your life in which you are lacking. When you fail to live
up to unrealistic standards, you create anger, depression, or both.
When you are depressed, however, you feel, "I can't do anything
right. Nothing works for me. I can't even be an average person."
The best time to work on perfectionistic tendencies is not on the
days you feel depressed, but at a time when you can be objective
about yourself.

As her therapy continued, Marilyn began to reexamine her
life. Starting at home, she became more attuned to the needs of
her husband and children. She appropriated time for family fun,
as well as time for herself. Realizing that the pace at which she
was working could result in burnout, she allowed time for herself
to rest and replenish her strength. She made a list of her priorities, and she began to pursue what appeared most important.

Within three months, Marilyn took a new direction.
Perfection was important, but completing a task and doing it
well were more important. A touch of humility made her interact with people with greater sensitivity.

She accepted herself as a human being with talents and
limitations. She was able to distinguish between two kinds of

limitations: those that come with selfhood and those that are imposed by other people. She had to figure out what was of importance to her.

All my life, I myself have struggled with the same issue—what is important? I wanted to be a writer. This was a constant need I felt within. My soul felt nurtured each time I finished a book. But writing did not pay the bills. I had to work for a living and pursue my writing ambition after my work day. This is what I am doing now, pursuing my passion that nurtures the soul. I love my life.

Perhaps you should ask yourself a realistic question: Do I have to be outstanding, excel in everything, be perfect, or should I pursue a life of balance where I experience contentment and peace?

In a recent session with Marilyn, I gave her a quotation from Maria Shriver's book, *Ten Things I Wish I'd Known Before I Went Out into the Real World*:

> *Perfectionism doesn't make you perfect. It makes you feel inadequate. You are not worthless because you cannot do it all. You are human. You can't escape that reality, and you can't expect to. Self acceptance is the goal. If Shakespeare were a Superwoman, she might have said, "To be or not to be—takes time and wisdom."*

Thoughts to Consider:

- During difficult times, faith and prayer pave the path that leads to God. In your own way, connect with him. In adversity there is blessing. Allow God to move into your life, yield to his voice as you read the holy scripture:

When anxiety was great within me, Your consolation brought joy to my soul. The Lord has become my fortress, and my God is the rock in whom I take refuge. He is the ultimate power, always available to those who patiently put their trust in Him. (Ps 94)

- In ambivalent times, when your plans are impeded or fail, remember, *the Lord knows our thoughts* (Ps 94:11) and has other plans for you—a new direction, a new point of view. It may be hard for your mind to perceive the idea that God is totally aware of your needs. You may wish to see quick and easy results. But God's special plan can only be perceived by faith, which is an activity of the heart. This requires patience, persistence, and prayer.

- Taking care of your soul, the immortal part of you, implies an ongoing awareness as you interact with the world around you, in thought, word, or action. Make each encounter—be it with your spouse, mate, child, sibling, friend, boss, colleague at work, and so forth—a spiritual contact. Instead of antagonizing those whose personality or opinion is different from yours, show them acceptance, compassion, respect. Each one of them has a soul that may need some of your attention.

Chapter 10

The Soul after Death

A season is set for everything, a time for every experience under heaven: A time for being born and a time for dying.

Ecclesiastes 3:1–2

After an elementary exploration of the soul, the spiritual aspect of our self, it may be of benefit to enter another intangible and sensitive area, the soul after death. Does anyone really know what happens to our soul after death? Theologians of the highest rank, scholars and prominent spiritual people who spent a lifetime studying holy scriptures and philosophical ideas, when confronted with the subject of death take a step back. They hesitate to be dogmatic about it, because no human knowledge can give an answer to the mystery of beyond. It is only faith that dissipates the shadows of doubt and allows our searching minds to soar higher and seek God's answer.

We are all aware that someday our physical self will cease to exist. The thought of dying is very scary to most people; to others it is a natural part of life: Eat, drink, and be merry, for tomorrow we die. Many dismiss or ignore the matter until an immediate relative or a close friend dies. *I don't mind dying, but when it happens I don't want to be there,* is a statement attributed to Woody Allen. Although humorous on the surface, on a deeper level it may possibly be a cover for his fear of death. Young people are concerned with their intimacies and future careers; most of the rest of us, besides being concerned about survival, are looking for answers to the questions: Is there a soul? Is there a life after life? Where would that be? What will take place after we die? The answers we give to ourselves design our current life. When philosopher Socrates was sentenced to die by poison, far from fearing death, he perceived it as his "ultimate reward."

For Plato, the soul is immortal. It preexists the body. It is conjoined with the body, and if it is nourished by philosophical activity, death will be its ultimate liberation. Plato considers the body, as mentioned in a previous chapter, *the prison of the soul.* In his view, the body is a source of pain, pleasure, and desire, which impede the search for truth. We attain truth only when the soul, upon death, separates from the body and from bodily senses. Then, according to Plato, the soul enters the world of ideas that are ultimate realities. These are of spiritual essence, and, therefore, immortal.

One may consider philosophical thought as more than an intellectual exercise. If it is used with good intentions, it may enable us to pursue an authentic spiritual life. This goal can have an incalculable impact on the course of our daily life as we practice and appropriate the teachings of Christ. Of course the question, *What happens after death to that part of self that keeps us alive,* must be answered even in a human limited way, for personal serenity and purposeful living.

In our attempt to make sense of the world, we cannot avoid thinking of events that lie ahead, especially that mysterious event when our human existence comes to an end. To deal with the question of afterlife means to accept the reality of death. Until we have fully accepted the fact that our death is real, there is no reason to consider whether or not there is an afterlife.

Our rational minds perceive birth and death as two ends of the same yardstick called life. Where there is life, there is death, we tell ourselves and dismiss the thought. The fear of death is a debilitating reality; it disrupts the unity of soul and body and the· union among beloved persons. The comforting thought for a spiritual person is the belief that death is the gateway to immortality. As the butterfly frees itself from its cocoon and enjoys a colorful field, likewise the soul frees itself from the body and finds everlasting joy in the presence of a loving God.

Christianity is particularly rich in this area and decisively defines that we possess a soul which never dies. Our death is not final. Upon death, the soul remains in a preliminary state, a foretaste of the age to come, when Christ will come in glory to judge and reward the living and the dead.

Our human perception of this reality is limited, just as our perception of Christ's presence in our life is limited. Here is where faith takes over to reassure us that, at the end of our days, God will raise our bodies from the grave and reunite them with our souls. Reconstituted as we were during our life span on earth, we will be brought before Christ to account for our lives and receive the appropriate reward or punishment. How can this be? Faith answers: If God created the universe out of nothing; if God created life and made humans his co-creators, would it be impossible for him to intervene in our human history and bring us back to life? If this life, in its pure form, is so beautiful, one can imagine what kind of life a loving God has prepared for his people.

Personally, I do not make any claim to be an authority on the subject of what will happen to me after I die; I can neither ignore the reality of death nor be preoccupied with it. How I deal with my death is crucial to how I deal with my life. This is what gives greater urgency to the issue of my soul after life. Perceiving the afterlife is not simply determining what will happen to me in some indefinite future; it affects how I live today. If my death is an integral part of the larger reality that constitutes my life, then to deal with my life demands that I do not ignore my death.

Oftentimes, especially when I am physically ill or unusual symptoms affect my well-being, disturbing thoughts cross my mind: What if this is it? What if I drop dead, right now while I'm writing this chapter? Oh God, please, don't let it happen yet; I need more time. I have so much unfinished business.

> Then my own mind interprets what God's response might be: All the "What ifs" can only stop you from living your present life. Some day you will die, and you will leave behind you unfinished tasks, because life is an unfinished business. But I have plans for you, as I have for all humanity. Trust that I am a God of the living.

I ponder the thought of dying and leaving behind my loved ones, leaving some of my intimate dreams and certain plans unfulfilled. Then, as if I have control over life and death, certain images haunt me for a little while, and I am reminded that I must come closer to our Lord Jesus Christ through prayer and decent behavior.

As I indulge in the projected future in a narcissistic fantasy, I beg the reader to see it simply as a personal image. I do visualize my departure time, especially the day of my funeral in the Greek Orthodox Church. Flowers, priests, clouds of fragrant incense, eulogies, tears, and chanting seem to interpret human pain. Melodic poetry and messages emerge from devout and warm hearts and rise straight to their own spiritual target, God.

The following is a small part of the funeral chant written by a monk of the East, John of Damascus (675–749):

> *Like a flower our human life withers, and like a dream*
> *it vanishes.*
> *But when we hear The Call, we shall all rise to meet*
> *the Lord*
> *And shall ever be in his Glorious, Loving and Sweet*
> *Presence.*
>
> *What earthly sweetness remains unmixed with grief?*
> *What glory remains immutable on earth?*
> *All mortal things are vanity, for they do not exist after*
> *death.*
> *Wealth does not endure, neither does glory accompany*
> *the deceased.*
>
> *All things are most feeble shadows, most deluding*
> *dreams.*
> *Once death comes, all human knowledge and glory*
> *vanish like vapor.*

Lord God, among your saints , rest the soul of your ser-
vant,
Whom You have chosen today, in a place where life is
eternal.

This dramatic scene has no affect whatsoever on my well-groomed body lying soulless in the coffin. I feel no sadness or pain; yet, in my soul, I am in full realization that this is the end of my earthly life, but at least, on this sad occasion, I am among most loving people, especially my family.

In my mind's eye, I see my wife Pat, my children, and grandchildren sitting in the front pew; they are inconsolable, pain shadowing their beautiful faces. Each one recollects sweet memories of the past. Periodically, they wipe their tears and feel a tinge of anger at the thought, *Why could he not have lived a little longer? I wish he were still with us.* In spite of their profound grief, I envision my children and grandchildren moving on with their individual lives; they have to, because they are young and full of vitality, and I am happy for them. Life is for the living, and it is my joy to see them advancing in life, making good choices, living long, and cherishing God's blessings while on earth. My eyes are fixed on my beautiful and loving wife. Dressed in total black and more beautiful than ever, she cannot control her tears. Hers is the greatest pain. She is losing her mate, the man that loved her so much, and whose love she returned in abundance. A lifetime of joyful as well as difficult experiences that she shared with me parade on the screen of her mind as she sighs.

How I wish to reach out even for a few moments and put my arms around her as in the past, soothe her pain, and reassure her that it is just fine where I am, no longer in my body, no more earthly concerns. I am happy in our Lord's presence, and at this hour he is invisibly near her, sharing her feelings. He will take her pain away and show her the direction she must take. Most of all, I want to tell her how grateful I am that she invested her wonderful youthful years with me—a life of love and respect that enriched my life as she stood by me in whatever good I was able to do. I also want to ask her to forgive me for any hurts or disappointments I might have caused her over the years by my words or actions.

Suddenly, the rays of the sun shine through the stained-glass window, rest on the altar screen, and pour bright light over an array of Byzantine icons. Between tears, Pat looks behind my coffin and sees the icons, a sign of hope. Christ on the right and his Blessed Mother on the left, Byzantine icons, sketches of divinity, underscoring the rule of eternity that awaits us all. I look at her tearful eyes and pray that the mercy of our Lord Jesus in his own compassion will provide comfort and healing for her aching heart. I wish I could say, *My love, your grief will eventually subside, life will continue, and you and our family will find comfort in your good memories of me.* But she cannot hear my words, for my voice and thoughts are silent; they can only be heard and known in her soul.

My eyes turn toward friends and acquaintances attending my funeral service. They are sad, but they comfort themselves in their thoughts, praising my virtues. *He was such a wonderful man…too bad he died so soon. He looks so much at peace! May God rest his soul.*

I take a second look at them and smile, tempted to say, *Knock it off, fellows. Be honest. I was not as good as you say. I was just as human as you are. But thanks anyway for being here today. Some day we may see each other in heaven. Meanwhile, continue to be present in my family's life. They may need your friendship.*

After the burial service, I see Pat, heartbroken and distraught, returning home from the cemetery and no longer finding me at my desk. With a feeling of awesome loneliness and isolation, she looks around—books, diplomas on the wall, icons, favored artifacts and souvenirs. Each corner of our house brings back memories of me. She picks up an album of family pictures, and old memories return. She looks at a picture of our youngest daughter, Katina, squeezed between our two bodies. We always called it the *Katina sandwich.* Another photo shows a closeup of the two of us dancing. She closes the album and smiles. I know why. I was never a good dancer, and she used to tease me about it. I'm sure, she remembers my reaction: *My love, you did not marry Fred Astaire or John Travolta; you chose to marry a former priest and now a psychotherapist who cannot dance—but he can write books!*

Tonight, she hopes at least to have a dream about me and perhaps hear my voice. She goes to our bed alone; she sighs; she can smell my scent among our pillows. Half-awake and half-asleep, she extends her hand and pretends to touch me—I am not there. The following nights are long and lonely. Loneliness at its worse seeps in to replace those intimate days together, events of celebration, holidays, births and birthdays, anniversaries, plans, and future travel. Our life together is over.

This is the day that death put a huge gap between us. I can see her agonizing as the options appear limited. She can no longer pray with the same fervor. She cannot go to our home sanctuary where she and I used to stand and pray each day. Of course she would be going back to church, but she would not be able to reach out as she used to at peak moments of the service, squeeze my hand and smile. How much I cherished her touch! It nurtured my soul.

As I realize that I cannot control the destiny of my loved ones from the coffin or from the grave, I let go of my images and face the real issue: *What will happen to me after death?* Now I'm totally aware that it is easier to indulge in fantasy and remain painfully passive than to write about the reality of death. Honestly, I do not know what my destiny will be after death. However, what my mind alone cannot fathom, my faith suffices as I turn toward a loving God, who intervened in human history and appeared in human form as the one, Jesus Christ. Being the author of life and death, in his caring love he has brought me this far in life, and, therefore, he will provide the answer.

One thing evident to all of us is that our body will eventually return to its elements. But what about that spirit in us, our soul? Death has no dominion over the soul.

By his death and resurrection, Christ destroyed death and gave life to those in the grave.

In John Chrysostom's words:

No one need fear death; the Savior's death freed us from it...death, where is your sting? Hades, where is your victory? Christ is risen and you are overthrown. Christ is risen and demons have fallen. Christ is risen and angels rejoice. Christ is risen and life rules. Christ is risen and not one dead remains in the tomb. This was also the conviction of those who witnessed Christ's resurrection and went out into a hostile world against all adversities to preach about it. Most of them suffered tortures and were put to a cruel death because of their faith in Christ.

Was Christ ever afraid of death? A quick look at the gospel narratives provides the answer. In the garden of Gethsemane, he said to his disciples:

> *I am deeply grieved, even to death. Remain here while I go over there to pray. He withdrew from them a stone's throw, knelt down and prayed: "My Father, if it is possible, let this cup pass from me; yet not what I want but what you want."* (Matt 26:38–40)

Obviously, in his human nature he felt the bitterness of the cup. He was a man of flesh and blood, living and breathing like one of us. Alone in the night, alone before God, he knew that his destruction was near. He would be mocked and scourged, and then his body would be pierced and nailed to a cross. Did he have any fear as he prayed?

> *In His anguish, He prayed more earnestly, and His sweat became like great drops of blood falling down on the ground.* (Luke 22:44)

We can assume that this was evidence of fear. As a man, he was afraid of the impending tragedy. But as God, he was not afraid. In his divine nature, he knew and reassured his disciples that he would rise in three days.

As we take an honest look at the death and resurrection of Christ, we feel the intensity of his life, his ability to live fully, to love completely, to be all that he came to earth to be. He was able to risk everything, to give himself away totally, and to enable his disciples to see in these qualities a doorway into eternity. The disciples entered this experience, and when they did, they felt resurrected; their eyes were opened and they saw that Jesus was alive, and also that he was one with God. He was the doorway to God, opening the way to all and inviting all to come, enter, live, love, be, and experience the joy of heaven. We wonder how it could be difficult for anyone to accept such a loving invitation, even as a personal challenge, and realize the teachings and values that Christ offers.

If there is no resurrection of the dead, then Christ has not been raised, and our faith is in vain. This was St. Paul's way of spelling out the relationship between Jesus' resurrection and our resurrection. In his first epistle to the Thessalonians, he reassures us that *we would be with the Lord forever.*

But one might ask: Well, who was St. Paul and why should I believe in what he claimed 2000 years ago? Good question, and it merits some attention. We need to start with someone with some evidence that we can trust: Saul the Jew, Paul the apostle—the man who crisscrossed the known world of his time, proclaiming the Gospel of Christ whom he never saw. Out of the dusty roads of Palestine, he traveled through Asia Minor and Greece to Italy, even to the Straits of Gibraltar, the storied "Pillars of Hercules." Before his encounter with the call from

Jesus on the road to Damascus, Saul persecuted the church of God violently and tried to destroy it. As a young man, he was trained by one of the greatest scholars in Jewish thought and culture. He understood the elements of the law and practiced them with zeal. Yet, his life changed dramatically when he came face to face with the cry from Jesus Christ as he traveled to Damascus, where he was going to cause more havoc among the believers. Then he heard that voice thundering from the sky, *Saul, Saul, why do you persecute me?*

Astounded, Saul replied, "Who are you, Lord?"

"I am Jesus, whom you are persecuting, but rise and enter the city, and you will be told what you are to do" (Acts 9:3–7).

He was told what to do by Ananias, a devout man of the area, and Saul was renamed Paul. But the gospel that he preached with passion to the sons of Israel and to the Gentiles was not his own. In his words, *I did not receive it from man nor was I taught it, but it came to me through a revelation of Jesus Christ* (Gal 1:11–12).

Back to Jesus. When Jesus met Martha whose brother had died and was four days in the tomb, some two miles away from Jerusalem, he said, "Your brother will rise again."

"I know that he will rise again in the resurrection day on the last day," she said.

Jesus replied, "I am the resurrection and the life. Those who believe in me, even though they die, will live, and everyone who lives and believes in me will never die."

At the tomb, Jesus wept—a most powerful statement about the *Theanthropos—the God-Man, Jesus.* The Jews present said, "See how much he loved him." Then Jesus brought Lazarus back to life in the presence of many witnesses. Possessed by fear and jealousy, some of the Jews plotted to kill him. The encounter of Jesus with the death and resurrection of Lazarus is recorded succinctly in the Gospel of John 11:1–44.

In Matthew's Gospel 25:31–46, we find a striking scene where Jesus speaks emphatically about his coming as the king in glory with all his angels to reward the righteous and sinners. Those who did good things in their lifetime, the ones who caringly provided for the needs of others — *Whatever good you did to one of the least of these who are my brothers and sisters, you did to Me* — he sent to eternal life. The others who were self-absorbed and did not care about anyone else's needs, he sent away to eternal punishment. The message of this chapter is evident. We do not look forward to reward or punishment alone; we are accountable before the Lord for the way in which we live our lives. Matthew also speaks about life after death. The righteous are blessed and inherit the kingdom, eternal life, and bliss. The wrongdoers go to eternal punishment. Today, there are Jews who believe that, at the end of days, the dead will be resurrected and come before God to account for their lives on Earth, that the righteous will be rewarded and the evil punished.

In Luke's Gospel 16:19–31, Jesus tells the story of the rich man and Lazarus, another story that gives evidence that our life continues after death.

> *Lazarus, the poor man, hungry and destitute, died and was carried away by angels to be with Abraham* — [in other words, he was in the presence of God]. *The rich man also died and was buried. Down in Hades* — [in

other words, he was deprived of God's presence]—
*where he was tormented, he looked up and saw
Abraham far away with Lazarus by his side.*

*He called out, "Father Abraham, have mercy on me,
and send Lazarus to dip the tip of his finger in water
and come to me to cool my tongue, for I am in anguish
in this flame." Abraham said, "Child, remember that
during your lifetime you received your good things, and
Lazarus in like manner evil things; but now he is comforted here, and you are in agony. Besides all this,
between you and us a great chasm has been fixed, so
that those who might want to pass from here to you
may not be able, and no one can cross from there to us."*

Death will happen to all of us someday. We are born and
we die. Birth and death represent the twin terminals of life. But
how do we integrate the reality of death into our understanding
of life? We live with the awareness that there was a beginning
and that there will be an end. We all know that we are dying; day
by day we come closer to our death. Each night we go to sleep
not knowing whether or not we will awaken in the morning.
When we awaken, we are grateful for another day. The best way
to deal with the issue of death is to live in a fully conscious, compassionate, loving way. We should not wait until we are on our
deathbed to recognize that this is the only way.

Within the temporal frame of life and death, we sense our
vulnerability. The universe around us manifests a generalized
order. Longingly, we marvel and speak about the accuracy of
laws and order of nature. The sun rises every morning and sets

every evening, and the seasons change on schedule. But hovering around the fringes of human existence is a barely suppressed sense of impending doom: illness, sudden deaths, natural disasters, economic distress, warfare, and acute awareness of alienation and vulnerability.

Does all this mean that death is the ultimate reality of human life? Would the mastermind of all creation and giver of life allow such a tragic end to the human being, the masterpiece of his creation? I do not believe so. But I do believe that Christ the healer of soul and body enables a person of faith to see beyond the grave with eyes of the soul. Truly, the soul leaves the body, but being of spiritual essence, it returns to its Creator. The last article of the Christian Creed says, *I look for the resurrection of the dead and the life of the ages to come.* As Christians, believing that Christ died on the cross, was buried, and came back to life, we anticipate an age in which we will be resurrected from the dead, and there will be no more death, pain, or sorrow, but life everlasting. Will we have a body, some identity of who we are in life after death? Yes!

We see evidence in the above-mentioned story of the rich man and Lazarus. After his death, the rich man, from a long distance, recognized who Abraham and Lazarus were. There is also evidence in the story where Jesus was transfigured on Mount Tabor and appeared in dazzling white clothes—perhaps a foreshadowing of his resurrection. His disciples saw him talking with Moses and Elijah. These two prophets died hundreds of years before the resurrection of Christ, and yet they had an identity that the disciples recognized. Remember what Peter said to

Jesus, *Rabbi, it is good for us to be here; let us make three tents, one for You, one for Moses, and one for Elijah.*

I will not add any more examples that show evidence to support our soul's destiny, that our life does not end with death. This whole subject merits the writing of another book. Having limited theological knowledge, it suffices to say that, like birth, death is another beginning of a different life. Jesus said, *We will be like angels in heaven.* Whatever this means, I believe that beyond the grave our life will continue, and our body is going to be of spiritual essence. Food, clothes, care, and a place to live will no longer be needed. So I will close this chapter with two personal episodes that forge my faith in the life to come and give me hope to enjoy what remains of my earthly life at this time.

The first episode: During my tenure as priest at St. Sophia Cathedral in Los Angeles, California, I performed hundreds of funeral services. But one experience stands out. In Pomona, more than an hour away from Los Angeles, Eudoxia, an elderly woman unknown to me, was sick. Her daughter Eleni called and requested holy communion for her mother. The Christian Orthodox faith requires confession before communion, so I asked the woman if she wished to confess. She nodded, *Yes.* The daughter Eleni, who took care of her mother, left us alone. Peacefully and in perfect clarity of mind, Eudoxia confessed what she considered were all of her sins. Then she paused. *My son who lives in Athens never comes to visit me…and I miss him.* This yearning left a bitter smile on her face. Reverently, she received holy communion and thanked me for the visit. *Father, if my son ever comes to America, please tell him that I loved him a lot.* I nodded, saying, *I will,* and prepared to leave.

She sang a strange line with a rather weak, yet sweet voice, *He is bright like the sun, comely and beautiful,* and she pointed her finger high in the air toward the left side of her bed. Between curiosity and wonder, I asked, *Who is bright like the sun?* With a radiant glow on her face, she said, *Don't you see him? He's right here.* I turn and looked. I saw nothing, but I heard myself whispering, *Woman, please pray for me.* I left.

More than an hour later, still wondering what Eudoxia thought she had seen, I arrived at my office. Venita, my secretary, anxiously met me at the door and said, *The woman that you just gave communion to died. Her daughter expects a call from you.*

Eudoxia's days ended with a humble funeral service; her daughter and a few attendants came to pay their respects. Did her story really end? Please bear with me for another minute. A year later, I was vacationing in Athens, Greece. One sunny day, I took a long stroll in a busy section, known as Omonia Square, which was swarming with thousands of people and heavy traffic. Casually, I stopped a young man and asked for information. I wanted to buy recent records of Greek instrumental music.

"Sir, do you see that big building on the next block, Lambropoulos Brothers—on the third floor you'll find a great collection of the latest records." Hurriedly he moved on his way. As I walked in the direction he pointed, I heard his voice again, "Mister, mister!" He approached me as he called. "I know a better place with better prices and good service. Look over there." He pointed. "Before you get to that fountain, turn right, walk one more block and you'll see a very narrow alley—very busy. The third store on the right is the place. You can't miss the green sign: Records."

I found the store. It was small and could hardly accommodate five customers. A middle-aged man wearing a black arm band, a sign of mourning, stood behind a small counter and politely took care of orders. I was last in line. I asked him to help me choose a few pieces of good music. He took a profound look at me and said, "You are not from Athens, are you?"

I shook my head, No, but I wondered what made him ask.

"I can tell from the way you speak. You are either from Australia or America."

"I'm from America," I said.

His face instantly changed color as he said, "I wanted to come to America and visit my mother. She lived there for the past ten years. Unfortunately she died almost a year ago." He took a deep breath. "I could not even go to the funeral—too far."

"I'm sorry to hear it," I said. "Where in America did your mother live."

"In California, but I don't know the name of the town." He hesitated and then pulled an envelope from his register and pronounced slowly, "Pomona, California."

"Pomona?" I asked with rising curiosity. "What was your mother's name?"

"Eudoxia, and my sister Eleni still lives there." He went on to show me a picture of his mother and sister, taken a few years before. I did recognize the two women immediately, but I was not exactly sure how to respond, until I saw the return address on the envelope.

"I know the town and have been there. I knew your mother," I said.

He pulled back and looked at me dumbfounded.

"I am the priest who performed your mother's funeral."

"You are a priest?" Now his shock was compounded not by what I told him about his mother but also by my appearance. In Greece a priest would be bearded and dressed in a long black cassock and tall hat. I was an American priest in civilian clothes. When he heard the rest of the story—how I was called to minister to his mother and what she had said about him, he put his arms around me and cried, "My mother must have sent you here to tell me about her last days."

For a long time I pondered this whole encounter. In the midst of a crowded Athenian street, I had asked a stranger to help me; he had sent me to a special little store where I had met the son of a woman who had died the previous year five thousand miles away! Two questions still linger in my mind? Was this just a coincidence? Did his mother from her heavenly home send me to bring some comfort to her son?

> The second episode: *With profound grief, last night I witnessed our mother's death. She died peacefully. Please pray for her eternal soul.* Kiki

This was a telegram delivered to my office some time ago. It was from my sister who lives in Greece. Almost immediately I called overseas. She answered the phone with evident sadness in her voice. "Oh, how I wish you were here," she whimpered. We talked extensively about Katerina: how good she had been as a mother to us, and we both recalled pleasant memories about her in our growing years. Three days after her burial, I saw my mother in a dream. She had the small body of an eight-year-old girl; there were no arms or legs that I could see, but she had a youthful and beautiful face, and she was dressed in white. I picked her up and realized she had no weight. She looked at me with a radiant smile and said, *My son, put me on that sofa.* She pointed with glowing eyes. *I am very happy where I am now.* It was an old sofa in Kiki's house where she always liked to sit and do needlepoint. As I sat her down, my dream ended.

Now, years later, I'm still in a quandary: Did my mind improvise such a dream to defuse my grief? Or was that a message informing me that after death our souls do receive new bodies that are no longer physical? I rather believe the second, and as I think of both episodes, my faith in a loving God is forged. Some day all of us will find the answers. What we now perceive is like looking through *a glass, darkly,* as St. Paul, claims, but in eternity our perceptions will be perfected, when we will see reality *face to face* (1 Cor 13:12).

Thoughts to Consider:

- The soul forms the body, yet it is itself without a body. It is a spirit. Once the body ceases to function totally, the soul, being a spirit, separates from the body. It may be hard for anyone to see the beauty of the soul, because of our involvements in the present world and thoughts that one day our life here on earth will end.

- As you embrace the potential that this life may not be the end but the beginning of another, in your own way you will arrive at a gradual awareness and realization that this world cannot possibly be the end. Then observe yourself within, how some of your humanitarian pursuits—goodness and beauty, justice and courage, friendship and loyalty, love and compassion—could bring you lasting joy.

- Suppose you have only three months to live. It is truly a negative thought. Apart from the most loving person in your life, who would you like to be with during this crucial period? A blood relative, an intimate spouse, or a friend? You know the answer. When you consider a parallel question about your inner self, your immortal soul, would you rather be connected with it? Before you continue with Step IV, read again slowly the chapters in Step III. They may reveal an awareness within you, a feeling of "this is not the end but a new beginning, a new birth into a spiritual life." Pay attention to your soul. It is the most precious part of your personality.

Authentic Spirituality

The realization that you are not only a physical being, but you are also a soul destined for eternity, may motivate you to explore the meaning of spirituality. Spiritual life for anyone, regardless of faith or cultural background, is the path a person chooses to follow in response to the soul within. It is a process of transformation whose purpose is to recover spiritual qualities, which are part of every human being. As you clear your path from obstacles and appropriate these qualities, you will experience the joy and meaning of your spiritual ascent.

Chapter 11

Spirituality

Spirituality is not only concerned with the promise of a future life, nor does it offer an easy way out of earthly trials and responsibilities. On the contrary, it summons us to action, making us aware that it is by our faith and deeds that we shall be evaluated. At the same time, it promises us divine assistance in the conduct of our present lives.

Emilianos Timiades

Spirituality is a part of our human experience. It is an inner yearning that seeks contentment beyond the physical world. Whoever you are, whatever your cultural, ethnic, or religious background, you have an awareness that besides your parents who caused your birth, another power above all powers gave you life and continues to give you life. This awareness is the essence of religion.

True spirituality aims at transforming a human being from the image into the likeness of God. His or her archetype and destiny are of heaven, in God's heavenly kingdom, with no expectations of reward for good deeds.

In the midst of a society contaminated by conflicts, arrogance, greed, mistrust, suspicion, and hatred, the spiritual person stands out like *a little god* on earth, a *microtheos*. Spirituality is not necessarily a lonely soul's "union" with the divine, as perceived by Western thought. It is, rather, a communal effort, an ever-present relationship with one another: God and neighbor. Authentic spirituality does not ignore the material world. It does not reject the body, pleasure, or material wealth, but it draws them into communion with the Holy Spirit. Our conflicts are not between body and spirit, but between our self imprisoned within versus our self open to a joyful state of *koinonoia*—fellowship— accepting, loving, and caring for the new life offered by God.

A spiritual person is gentle and kind, a healer, a friend to all and a fountain of wisdom, embodying peace and spreading joy. He or she sees in the inmost part of the other person the image of God, though the other may hold differing opinions, beliefs, or attitudes.

Whether you are a Christian, Muslim, Jew, or Buddhist, spirituality is not a destination at which you ultimately arrive. It is a way of life in which you and I strive to become aware of God's presence and purpose in our lives and in everything visible around us. It is a realization that *the Earth is the Lord's and the fullness thereof.*

Visualize a high mountain and a number of people eager to climb it. The challenge to reach the top fascinates everyone, and yet each mountaineer chooses his or her own path. In your effort to remove yourself from the everyday material world and attain a higher, spiritual plane, you have to choose your own path.

The path to spirituality is neither smooth nor straight. Following the trail requires intelligent action and reverent understanding. It is not a matter of blind faith; it is not a passionate practice of a religion. It is an issue with a purpose, if only from the perspective of an inner yearning to meet God.

God earnestly awaits us, ready to speak to us the word of truth, the only redeeming, liberating, and saving word. The soul, pressed by all thoughts that stem from this present misleading world, cannot fully know God. St. Basil, a devout and dedicated man of the fourth century, reminds us that we need:

> ...to take time and distance from all these material and temporary attractions, so that we may begin to know God. Taming of the passions will enable us to acquire serenity and the necessary elements to build a life near God. Having found peace again, and no longer being allured by any external attractions, the soul repossesses itself like a clean mirror which does not tolerate any stain.

"Oh God!" Notice how in our daily conversations, pleasant or unpleasant, God's name is mentioned. This yearning for God becomes more pronounced in difficult times. When things do not go well, when we fall ill and feel pain, when we are in dire need and have exhausted all known resources, we lift our eyes high toward something invisible.

"Oh, God, where are you? Please help me!" is the cry of a human in pain. We expect God to be available when we need him. We expect him to be in the ambulance on our way to the emergency room. When we prosper, however, and the wind is favorable to our sails, we ignore him or pay him lip service. That is not loving God; that is using God.

On that dreadful and memorable day when the World Trade Center was attacked, many people raised serious questions: How could a God of love allow such a heinous act of destruction? Where was God and why did he remain distant? These and similar agonizing questions crossed our minds, causing doubt and disbelief. We have no viable answers. Our wounded souls continue to seek healing.

Accidental deaths, earthquakes, hurricanes, tornadoes, crime, and poverty are not God's actions against humans. They are aspects of life, as are sunny days, cloudless skies, calm seas, compassion, and prosperity. When human doubt surfaces and asks the disturbing question, *Where is God?* at best we can rely on scriptural support that reassures us that God's ways are not our ways. He loves us better than we love ourselves. He gives us freedom and does not interfere with our choices, lest he deprive us of our dignity as his children.

When human tragedies occur, it is not God that wills them. The God of love, forgiveness, and reconciliation does not will tragedy, death, and destruction. The evil inclination that lurks in the human heart causes some people to make choices that result in such loss. Power and control over others, jealousy and greed take charge and fuel the evil proclivity in humans and bring about catastrophe.

When human tragedy of any kind occurs, the ever-present Christ is again crucified. He is there bleeding, along with the victims of evil and hatred. He is there in full agony, co-suffering and consoling, healing and loving. In the silence of dark days, he interprets and repeats their painful cry, "Eli, Eli, Lama Sabachthani," found in Psalm 22:1–5, which means "My God,

my God, why have you deserted me?" Like Christ in his humanity, we feel that God is absent when we are in pain or on the
brink of death. In a crisis of illness or death, or terrorism and war,
we are confronted with the serious question, *Where is God?*
Stricken by sadness or despair, our first and visible response is
negative: Does God really exist? If he does, where is he now that
we need him? It is at these crucial moments that we are challenged to convert our protest against the absurdities of our
human condition into a prayer. Truly a hard task! But out of the
depths of our pain, we lift our eyes, whimper and whisper words
of prayer to him who holds our life in his hands and heart with
infinite love and mercy.

Where else can we go? Where can we find true comfort
and healing? Who can really understand how we feel? At best,
we consider contacting a friend who could genuinely listen.
There is a therapeutic effect in talking to a friend who is willing
to share our feelings. His or her words, simple though they may
be, can soothe our pain even for a little while. And the moment
we feel some relief, we can return to our prayer. "Focus unto the
Lord...keep your eyes fixed on Christ (Heb 12:1). This initial
phone call to a friend is a positive step. Isolating ourselves and
not wanting to see another human being is negative.

The practical effects of communion with God are seen in
our daily behavior. The way we think, feel, and interact with
other people precipitates our disposition. When our character
and relationships are shaped by biblical teachings, we gain stability, consistency, and purpose in life. These spiritual fruits indicate that Christ lives within our heart. He is immovably,
everlastingly, continuously accompanying a hospitable soul.

How many of us totally understand the laws that govern the stars, the sun, the moon, and the many galaxies and the order and motion of the universe, the beauty of nature, the marvelous rhythm of cosmic flow, and the functions of our own bodies? Although all are basically physical in scale, they are also deeply spiritual in content, for they point to God the Creator and Sustainer of the Universe.

We believe and take it for granted that the sun will rise tomorrow as it has for millions of years. Who directs the flowers to give fragrance and the plants and trees to yield fruit? Who or what power maintains the life of the universe? As we take a glimpse at nature—the thousands of flowers of different shades originating from one source of light, the size and shape of different trees nurtured by the same soil—we can gratefully share the psalmist's enthusiasm: "How magnificent are Your works, O Lord; in wisdom You have created everything."

Human beings seek in their own way to make themselves more noble and to realize their own true worth. As we connect with people, observing the shade and shape of their appearance, listening to their different languages and pronunciations, viewing their customs, religious orientations, and political persuasions, we realize that we all originate from the same essence, from the same God who sustains and loves us. We have the same needs, and each of us deserves respect and a good life. While we appreciate the many physical manifestations of humanity, we marvel at God's creative wisdom. One has to take a deeper look to realize how God's creative power is manifested through each one of us.

We admire the accomplishments of our scientists today. The great minds of our times work diligently in laboratories to make our world a better place in which to live. We are grateful knowing that contemporary technology makes human life easier. Human minds are God's workmanship.

If you are an artist committed to the pursuit of your talent, whether you are aware of it or not, your art is a manifestation of your spiritual self, for it connects your soul with its Creator, who is the ultimate artist.

If you are a scientist determined to discover the cure for a malignant disease, or if you are in search of the truth about methods of improving living conditions, your motivation is one of spiritual origin, for all truth is in God.

If you are an average person working for a living and minding your own and your family's well-being, you are laboring in God's vineyard, fulfilling a purpose in life that is as important as every other contribution.

If your purpose is to serve the well-being of others, your efforts carry spiritual overtones for they are inspired by the giver of all good things. You are already a spiritual person; you are expressing God's love.

Relax your mind for a few minutes. Remain still and silent. Allow your soul to become the guiding force in your life. Enjoy the ecstasy of God's creation. Even if you fail to understand how so many things transpire in your life, surrender and accept them. Surely, resistance may hold you back. To doubt is human, to believe is divine, and for a precious moment, shift from doubt to faith.

When you start combating resistance, which could represent your own personal shortcomings, life can get more difficult before it becomes more coherent and tranquil. A great deal depends on what aspects of life you have been ignoring. A major part of spirituality is concerned with those qualities of the human spirit—love and compassion, tolerance and forgiveness, contentment, responsibility, harmony—that bring happiness to both self and others.

When you become a compassionate, loving, patient, tolerant, and forgiving person, you will recognize the potential impact of your actions on others and how such influence shapes their conduct. Think of Christ's act of forgiveness from the cross. He had the power to destroy his crucifiers with a thought. Instead, he acknowledged their spiritual ignorance. "Let them go," he said, "for they know not what they do." Demonstrating God's love, he sought to awaken the spiritual within his persecutors. Christ accomplished more through loving forgiveness than could ever be accomplished through a destructive force. Such is the power of spiritual law. It works, it endures, and ultimately it helps us to improve our daily affairs.

In your struggle to get to know and accept yourself, inevitably you will encounter certain issues that will evoke insecure feelings. However, your patience, persistence, and perseverance will be rewarding. During this time of your life, becoming involved with your faith, attending church, temple, or mosque, reading a good book, talking to a spiritual friend or to an experienced religious person can bring forth a rediscovery of your spiritual self.

Some day our physical self will be no more—I pray it will occur after we reach an old, old age. Perhaps we will rest beneath a tombstone engraved with our date of birth and our date of death. There will be no record of our soul's existence. Our soul never dies. Knowing this, that our life continues after death, leaves no room for doubt of the importance of pursuing our personal spirituality. As you contemplate the concepts above, connect with your soul and let this process become important in your present life.

Thoughts to Consider:

- Every human being wishes to be happy, seeks ways of fulfillment, gratification, and joy. Many people try hard to remove the clutter, restore the good, bring order and beauty into their lives and be good to others. Such efforts pave the way toward a more rewarding life.

- Whoever you are, wherever your life is today, however much you have, you may thirst for more—a better job, more money, a more loving mate, something happier, prettier, richer, tastier, or more satisfying. No matter which category you fall into, your basic need is the same as any other person's: a life of essence and of meaning, an experience where the ever-presence of God is felt.

- A dark room can be illumined to some degree with candles and lanterns, but with the flick of an electrical switch, the room can be flooded with light. The power of electricity makes it possible, and makes our lives brighter. Likewise, God's power, which sustains the universe and makes life possible, can enrich and enlighten your life.

Chapter 12

Purification

> *Our cultural conditioning makes spiritual discipline*
> *and effort very difficult. Society says, "If you are stressed,*
> *have a drink, take a drug, or install yourself in front of*
> *the television. That will help you to relax." If you are*
> *honest with yourself, however, you know in your heart*
> *that these techniques are not the real answer.*
>
> Jack Canfield

Keep your body, mind, and heart healthy. They need to be in harmony if you are to explore a more spiritual life. Your body, this wonderful vehicle that God has given you for your earthly travel, requires regular exercise and rest, healthy nutrition and proper care. Most people feel ready to face the world after their daily bath or shower. A well-kept, manicured body promotes optimum performance. In general, good grooming and daily washing keep our bodies healthy. Other people who cross your path may feel pleased with your neat appearance. *Cleanliness is wealth*, claims an old saying. Keeping a house clean or a working area tidy makes life more pleasant. You may feel proud when your car is freshly washed and polished. People who own boats take them out of the water once in a while to remove the barnacles so that the boat may sail freely. Before a physical examination, a cleansing of your intestines is required. Wounds must be thoroughly swabbed as part of the healing treatment. We believe it is beneficial to our health to purify our drinking water. Cleansing and purification are important for your physical well-being, and they promote health and energy. Your body makes you aware of its needs, and should you require help to meet those needs, the market can supply nutrition and diet books that provide ample information about ways to develop and maintain a healthy physical condition.

Your body needs a secret habitat where you can maintain a life of reasonable comfort, peace, and vision. This state of being cannot be attained if your home is cluttered with things, gadgets that you are keeping "just in case." You tell yourself, "This or that may come in handy some day." Many of the items we accumulate are nothing but neurotic attachments—an old chair, an antique lamp, grandmother's needlepoint—that help to defuse our anxiety about life's adversities. These attachments infer lack of trust in a caring God who can provide for your needs, and you may feel insecure and vulnerable.

Truly, there is something immensely therapeutic about clearing out clutter. While you are clearing out things on an external level, there is a corresponding cleaning going on internally. What is outside is always inside and vice versa. Being free of clutter is one of the greatest aids to attaining the life you want. Such freedom is essential if you truly want to experience more joy, less stress, and more happiness in your life. Your attachment to "stuff" consumes precious energy that could be used for fun or for creativity.

Removing the clutter in the mind requires the ability to conceive, perceive, and precipitate action. It is with the mind that you see; it is with the mind that you perceive. If the mind is clear, you see clearly. If it is blurred or confused, vision suffers. There can be no peace if the mind is inundated with fantasies, delusions, and erroneous ideas. Messages given to your mind by your five senses need to be mentally processed and properly appropriated. Practicing caution and prudence promotes a healthy, personal life for yourself and encourages happy interaction with other people.

The problems confronting the world today are numerous, urgent, and difficult; they are in need of well-thought-out spiritual direction. The struggle against inner dissatisfaction, troubled relationships, mental illness, and moral decadence requires the best effort we can give. We are capable of attaining spiritual greatness, but we are in dire need of models to inspire us. Where are they? We know where they are not. We certainly will not find them in front of a television set or in a bar or within pages of scandalous magazines. We live in a technological age that puts its faith in the perfection of the computer and electronic devices. Human beings tend to become like the god they worship, but fortunately for us who hold on to our faith, our agony does not allow us to become robots. The present generation is a bridge attempting to make a giant stride into spiritual realms. Faced with nuclear and biochemical weapons, faced with the possibility of our own self-destruction, we are trying to reconnect to the roots that have lain dormant underground for centuries, in the hope that genuine faith in a loving God may somehow counterbalance the sterility of the perfect machine. Most of us have no role models. Although we may have loved our homes and our families or admired the rich and famous, we have to be ruthlessly honest in evaluating our heritage. We have the choice to return to the holy scriptures and documents of dedicated people who gave form and shape to the Christian faith. St. Basil (329–388), suggests:

> *Let us listen to the words of truth which have nothing to do with controversial human wisdom, but are spoken by inspiration of the Spirit. Their aim is not to attract the praise of their listeners, but to effect their salvation.*

With a receptive mind, respect, and faith in the Creator and Sustainer of the Universe, you will rediscover the good sources that nurture the soul. St. Isaac the Syrian says:

> *Faith that God **will** act is essential. "As you have believed, let it be done unto you." It is an experience of grace which happens to those who are simple of heart and fervent in hope. Simplicity means, among other things, to avoid trying to explain or analyze what you feel about God in purely intellectual terms.*

Spiritual people live in the world in the hope of final victory of the powers of this age. In the fullness of time, all life will be transformed beyond imagining. This is expressed in the Bible as *a new heaven and a new earth*. This transformation is not a completion of our human plans and goals, but of God's.

Keep your heart pure. *Blessed are the pure in heart for they shall see God*, Jesus said. What is a pure heart?—a heart free of possessiveness, a heart capable of forgiving, a merciful heart, a loving heart, a heart that sees the other, not as a subject to be used but as a child of God to be respected.

By *human heart* I mean not the organ that pumps blood through the body but the unseen storehouse of emotions and feelings. *Create in me a clean heart, O God, and put a new and right spirit within me,* cried King David when the prophet Nathan brought him to the realization that he had committed two grave sins: adultery and murder. When the king looked inward, what did he find in his heart? Passion, power, lust, hardness and coldness of heart, desiring to do whatever felt good for his own flesh. Acknowledging his crime, he turned to God with a penitent mind and a humble heart, and said:

> *I know my transgressions, and my sin is ever before me.*
> *Against you, you alone, have I sinned, and done evil in*
> *your sight…restore in me the joy of your salvation.*
> *Purge me with hyssop, and I shall be clean; wash me*
> *and I shall be whiter than snow.*

In the Book of Psalms, we realize King David's transformation. He made strenuous efforts to control his thoughts and the dispositions of his heart. When he felt forgiven and reconciled with God, he said, *My soul is as peaceful as a child sleeping in its mother's arms.*

Stories, such as the following, verify that transformations in people occur even in our times.

One evening, Abbot Jonah of St. Katherine's Monastery at Mount Sinai asked Brother Benjamin, a middle-aged monk, how he had spent his day.

"Like all days," replied the monk. "I was very busy, and if God hadn't helped me, I wouldn't have done anything significant."

"What did you do?" the abbot asked.

"You would think I was an animal trainer; every day I guard two hawks, I control two roebucks, I train two hunting dogs, I get rid of a snake, I tame a bear, and I take care of a sick person."

Scratching his beard in wonder, the abbot said, "What are you talking about? We have no such jobs in this place."

"You're right," the monk replied. "However, I'm dealing with all these tasks daily. The two hawks are my eyes; I have to be constantly alert so my eyes will not look at obscene sights. The two roebucks are my feet, whose steps I must constantly observe lest they lead me in an evil direction. The hunting dogs are my two hands, whose purpose is to work and do whatever is good. The snake is my tongue, which I need to restrain so it won't engage in idle gossip or pour venom on my brothers. As for the bear, it is my own heart, which I must tame and discipline against pride and vainglory. The sick person is my vulnerable body; it is my responsibility to keep it healthy and clean from any abuse or lustful involvement."

Amazed at the monk's simple wisdom, the abbot said, "You should be the abbot here." He handed the monk his pastoral staff and said, "From now on, you're in charge of this monastery." The abbot, an austere and arrogant man who ruled the lives of the monks according to the letter of the law, felt his heart melting as he realized that this monk had God's teachings in his soul and a mission in life. The abbot experienced an inner transformation and returned himself to the rank of a simple monk.

To maintain good emotional health and bring peace and joy to your life, you must observe the thoughts that linger in your heart. If angry thoughts abide in your heart, you become more angry. If you harbor greedy thoughts in your heart, you become more greedy. If you entertain negative thoughts, you become a more negative person. Your life will move as the heart directs. However, an effort to refine and purify your thoughts will enable you to feel closer to God. Feeling closer to God instills peace in your soul. Inner peace, prayer, purity, humility, compassion, and godly life allow noble souls to feel the presence of God. The pure in heart can see God.

"Show me your God," demanded Autolykos, an atheist in the early church history.

Theophilos of Antioch (318–325) responded:

Just as those who see with the eyes of the body observe the affairs of earthly life, distinguishing things that differ, whether light or dark, so in the case of the eyes of the soul, it is possible to look at God. For God is seen by those who are able to see Him. Just as those who are wholly or partly blind fail to see the light of the sun, so do we have our eyes covered by our errors and evil actions. When there is rust on the mirror, it is not possible to see one's face in the mirror. Likewise, when the soul is tarnished by sin, such a one cannot see God.

The aim of spiritual life is the union of the human will with the will of God. This is the true miracle—a mystical experience that can help or hinder the achievement of this goal. There are several ways by which the mind can experience an ecstasy. Religious exercises and contemplation—Christian and non-

Christian—can produce that feeling of absolute peace and tranquility within. In our times, sex and romantic love are valued high above most affections precisely because of their ecstatic character, yet as important aspects of life as they can be, they are temporary. The mystical moment, however, is the spark that ignites the divine grace. Perhaps, this is another new beginning for you; it is worthwhile considering.

Do not be afraid or anxious. Enter eagerly into the treasure house that lies within you, and so you will see the treasure of heaven, for the two are the same, and there is but one single entry to them both. The ladder that leads to the kingdom within is hidden within you, and is found in your heart. Dive into yourself, and in your heart you will discover the rungs by which to ascend.

Theophan the recluse claims:

> The Kingdom of God is born in us when the mind is united with the heart. Then wandering of thoughts will cease, and you will gain a rudder to steer the ship of your soul, a lever by which to set in movement all your inner world. But how can one unite mind and heart? Acquire the habit of praying these words with the mind in heart, "Lord Jesus Christ, Son of God, have mercy upon me." Grafted to your heart, this simple prayer will lead you to the end which you desire. It will unite your mind with your heart and will give you power to govern the movements of your soul.

The Greek Orthodox mystics of the fifth century were convinced that God could only be known by a mind and heart that had been cleansed of all distracting thoughts and images. By systematically weaning their minds and heart away from their "passions"—such as anger, jealousy, judgment, greed, pride, and sadness, which tied them to earthy life—they would transcend themselves and become deified like Jesus on Mount Tabor, transfigured by the divine "energies."

Where you are at this moment—caring and nurturing body, mind, and heart—is a steady process of spiritual unfolding. It cannot be rushed or forced along, any more than a flower can be forced to bloom or a tree to yield fruit. Divine grace is given as a gift from the hand of God, as part and parcel of your relationship with him. God is the Lord, the giver of every good and perfect gift. The Father of all things visible and invisible knows your needs better than you do.

St. Basil confirms our relationship with God in a pithy prayer:

> *Lord, Lover of Humans, out of your love you created man and woman and honored them with your own image and likeness. You placed them in Paradise, promising life eternal and the enjoyment of good things in keeping your commandments. But when they disobeyed you, the true God, you banished them from Paradise. Yet in the midst of their corrupted life, you did not turn yourself away from them, but in different times through compassion and mercy you visited them, one generation after another. You spoke to them through the mouths of prophets and holy people, challenging their wrong-doings, guiding and pointing them*

the way to their salvation. And when the fullness of time came, you spoke to us by your Son. Although he was God from the beginning, in time he appeared on earth, taking on the human form—teaching, forgiving and healing—to restore humans to their original glory. He finally gave up his life to redeem people of their transgressions.

It is with faith, respect, and humility that you can explore these words of wisdom, which, when rightly applied, open up new horizons, closer to the giver of all good things.

Thoughts To Consider:

- *Complete serenity of mind and heart is a gift of God; but this serenity is not given without our own intense effort. You will achieve nothing by your efforts alone; yet God will not give you anything, unless you work with all your strength and pray with all your heart and mind to attain it. This is an unbreakable law.* (St. Makarios of Egypt)

- *The kingdom of heaven is within you. Within you are the riches of heaven, if you desire them. However sinful you may feel, the Kingdom of God is within you. Enter into your heart, seek more eagerly and you will find it. Outside of you is death, and the door to death is sin. Enter within yourself and remain in your heart, for there is God.* (St. Ephraim of Syria)

- *God is present as we reach out. It is not enough to render a social service in terms of money or to offer whatever help you can to some poor person in order to be considered a generous, merciful friend of the poor. Before any action, before opening your hands, it is necessary first to open your heart and feel sympathy and concern for the other.* (St. John Chrysostom)

Chapter 13

Letting Go

When you are not distracted by your own negative thinking, when you do not allow yourself to get lost in moments that are gone, you are left with this moment which can make the difference in your life. Truly, this moment is the only moment that you have.

Sydney Banks

A major part of the purification process is the decision to *let go*. Letting go of our past is one of the most difficult challenges in life. Like a dark shadow, events of the past follow us daily, preventing us from seeing that each day is a gift that could be cherished. Intellectually, we know that our past experiences, especially unhappy ones, cannot be changed; we keep recollecting them, knowing that they consume precious energy.

King David said, *For I am well aware of my iniquity, and my sin is before me always.* Memory, God's gift, tends to be an enemy when it gravitates around all the wrongs that we have done, the hurts and injustices that others have inflicted upon us, and the lack of recognition it gives to our good behavior.

Dwelling on a painful event is a type of self-inflicted wound, a self-flagellation, in which our attention and energy are focused on the thoughts: *Why did this happen to me? It was unfair. It should not have happened.* Thus, recovery and healing are prevented.

Why not visualize letting go as a transformation—moving from a dark night to the dawn—when you can see that self-made obstructions litter your path. This process requires a willingness to shed our persona—those unauthentic trappings we may be carrying with us because they are familiar, and yet we know they no longer serve any purpose. Choosing to let go will set us free to enjoy a new dimension of our lives.

In your personal life, whatever issues cause disappointment, once you leave the dark aspects of your past behind, you will be reminding yourself of the precious truths that you might have long known. Your soul will feel revitalized each moment when self-judgment fades away and self-compassion enters your thoughts. Healing of hurts and self-inflicted wounds begins the moment we clear away fear and negative thinking that weakens the soul. In Robert Frost's words:

> *Something we were withholding made us weak*
> *Until we found it was ourselves.*

Think of cultivating a spiritual life in the way Praxiteles created the classic statue of *Hermes with the Infant Dionysus.* As a sculptor, he knew that a perfect statue of a human body could be fashioned out of a huge piece of marble. He visualized the object of his creation and painstakingly chiseled away at that marble.

You, as a sculptor of your personality, can visualize the image of a spiritual person that will gradually emerge from your current life. The chipping away takes time and patience. You cannot attain a state of spirituality within a short period. It is important that you start the process patiently at this moment by removing carefully the wrongs, the negatives, and the destructives.

How?

How did the sculptor do it? What sensory organ did he use when he visualized the statue in the block of marble? It could be the inner eye, the awareness of his soul, or his creative intelligence. Whatever it was, it spoke of God's gift, the human ability to perceive and create. The sculptor's story speaks to us about the potential we have not even dreamed about that exists within each person.

You be the sculptor for a moment. This moment—now—accept the challenge. It is a beautiful and special moment for you. Like a colorful mosaic, your life can be a series of such moments to be experienced one right after another, creating the image that God meant for you. If you attend to each moment, you are already in the commonwealth of spiritual life.

Remember, you are God's masterpiece. *He has created you anew in Christ Jesus, so that you can do the good things He planned for you from the beginning* (Eph 2:10).

Take a thorough look and notice what went into the making of who you are today. You have probably internalized positive and negative and even mixed messages that you received from your parents and other significant adults in your life. Some of these messages surface unconsciously into your world today and influence your thoughts. You may realize that actions, behavior, comments of others throughout your childhood years have had an impact upon your personality. But now, you are in charge, and you can convert past influences into positive behavior.

Do you ever find yourself not trusting important people in your life? Are you impatient or short-tempered? Do you accept a compliment gracefully? Do you talk loudly? Are you obnoxiously persistent? Do you want to have things your way? If any of these questions are pertinent to your behavior, then proceed with another question: Where did you learn to respond this way? Obviously, like anyone else, you have had programming during your formative years.

Now you can put all negative memories in perspective. If a specific memory is still nagging you and affecting your current life, then drastic surgery is needed to remove it. You may ask the master sculptor who gives shape and form to our lives, the Holy Spirit, to work within you.

When you make your request in prayer, make sure that you sit patiently and quietly, allowing free-floating thoughts to surface in your mind. As you process these thoughts, you are not looking to parents, teachers, siblings, or relatives to blame for your feelings. You are looking for your own way to allow the artistry of the Holy Spirit to correct the blemishes.

An old prayer could serve as a starter:

Heavenly King, Comforter, the Spirit of Truth, everywhere present and filling all things, Treasury of Blessings and Giver of Life, come and dwell in me and cleanse me of every stain and save my soul, gracious One.

As certain painful past memories are filtered by the spirit that abides in you, you will sense the first step toward freedom.

For you, this can be a unique opportunity to be free from the control of the past. Like a child, your first steps may be halting and tentative. Attempting too much at once could discourage you. Yet as you develop new thoughts and ways of behaving, you will gain skill and strength to confront additional areas.

For example, take any painful memory. The intensity of the hurt may be so real that you have a hard time in letting it go. Part of you would like to avenge or retaliate; another part wants to forgive. Do you really want vengeance? To forgive might be easier and more productive, although it has been said that nobody seems to be born with much talent for forgiving. We all need to learn from scratch, and the learning almost always runs against our grain. However, as you think about letting go each day, the intensity of hurt will gradually diminish. Soon it will be no more than a historical event that has no influence on your present life.

God desires to meet us. Vaster than the universe, God is the source and goal of all that exists. He is the most loving one to whom all belong, upon whom all depend, and for whom we all long. God can be felt, though never seen or analyzed. The believer who senses God's presence and greatness becomes ecstatic in wonder, love, and praise.

God expresses himself in creation. Like a friend, he makes himself known by his actions and daily blessings that he bestows upon the world. He speaks through the scriptures, through the prophets, through holy and humble people, through all that is pure. Listen to that mystical voice with the ears of your soul. Although he is infinite and beyond all imagining, in his relationship with us he is very personal, very intimate. Those who live in intimacy with God are sometimes granted favors and blessed with certain privileges and gifts, such as healing power, inspiration, and a desire to do good for others. God grants these exceptional activities as lights in the darkness, to confirm his presence among his people, and to rekindle spiritual awareness and faith.

St. Paul's statement confirms God's love for us:

> *God sent his Son, born of woman, born under the law,*
> *to redeem those who were under the law, so that we may*
> *receive adoption as sons and daughters.*

God wants sons and daughters, not slaves, because he loves us. He respects the free will of his children, as seen in the case of the prodigal son's departure. And as we see in the prodigal son's return, we humans can overcome our weak nature, and we can change with God's help.

If you and I assume that because we have failed God— either by our lack of faith or disobedience or bad behavior and crooked life—he will not accept us, we will be limiting God's unconditional love. God has the ability to forgive. He has the ability to turn our failures into triumphs. He is able to heal our lives, restore us, put us back together, put us back on track. He is able to figure out a place that is just right for our particular personalities, strengths and weaknesses, talents and gifts. Furthermore, he desires to put you and me to use in his kingdom. Let's trust him to do it!

John Chrysostom shakes us into realization of what kind of God we have, in view of our sins. In his homily, he states:

> *God desired a harlot; and how does He act? He does*
> *not send to her any of His angels or archangels. No, He*

Himself draws near to the one He loves. He does not bring her to Heaven, but He comes down to earth, to the harlot, and is not ashamed. He visits her secret house and finds her in her drunkenness. And how does He come? Not in the bare essence of His original nature, but in the guise of one whom the harlot is seeking, in order that she might not be afraid when she sees Him, and will not run away to escape Him. He comes to the harlot as a man. And how does he do this? He is conceived in the womb, He grows little by little, as we do in a human body, that she may understand Him. He finds this harlot thick with sores and oppressed by devils. How does He react? He draws near to her. Afraid, as she sees Him, she is about to run away. He calls her back saying, "Why are you afraid? I am not a judge, but a physician. I come not to judge you but to save you." She comes back and is transformed. He takes her and espouses her to Himself, and gives her the signet-ring of the Holy Spirit, as a seal between them.

This metaphor is one of the most convincing statements of God's unconditional love for a corrupt and disturbed society. It is also a personal reassurance to a fallen human being who considers himself or herself sinful and unworthy. God's response is different from our human perceptions.

It is of great significance that God never imposes love and grace on the human will. He seeks our consent. When we consent, we cooperate with the whole will, heart, and spirit. This is the beginning of spiritual life, a most beautiful and rewarding mystery.

Human greatness is not an accomplishment of our own creativity but it is in our resemblance to the Creator. God continues his creation through us. Man or woman is "self-governed," ruled by his or her own will, in the image of the one who rules over all. We depend on God's assistance. We are "referential" beings who must continuously refer to God for help and guidance.

Thoughts to Consider:

- Do you find yourself dwelling on negative experiences from the past, believing that doing this actually enhances your healing and makes you a better person?

- Self-exploration is an important component of spiritual growth. Yet the opportunity to know our soul's potential may evoke scary feelings, because we associate spirituality with having to change.

- Although change is constant and inevitable, we prefer to turn our attention to the prevention of change in our lives, for change requires awareness and responsibility. We rarely think that tending to our soul's needs and becoming more spiritual might be an exciting and worthwhile adventure.

Chapter 14

The Art of Fasting

*Whenever you fast, do not look dismal like the hyp-
ocrites, for they disfigure their faces so others may see
that they are fasting.*

*Let your fasting be a secret. And your Father who
sees in secret will reward you.*

Matthew 6:16

Fasting is a physical discipline that strengthens our spiritual
self. It is highly significant to notice the first statement Christ
makes about fasting. He emphasizes the question of motive. He
does not say, *if you fast,* but rather, *whenever you fast.* He presupposes that we understand fasting as an important part of our
lives. We hear people talking about fasting; most of us know
about wholesome diets as an important aspect of a healthy life.
Physical health can be impaired by eating too much or too little.
A well-balanced diet promotes well-being and energy, life and
vigor, and an alert mind.

Athletes abstain from certain foods and stimulants, as do
scholars in times of strenuous mental work. Travelers, chroni-
cally ill people, and young children are not expected to follow
the practice of fasting. It is interesting to note that fasting is one
of the oldest health rules found in many philosophies and in all

religions, including the Christian faith. It has generally been considered a spiritual exercise.

The important issue is not what we abstain from, but what the purpose of our fasting is. How easy it is to try to use fasting to get God to do what we want. If that is the way we view the subject, how, then, are we to understand the statement in the Lord's Prayer that says, *Thy will be done?* To use religious practices for ulterior motives is always the sign of faulty faith. Some of us are tempted to believe that if we endure a period of strict fasting, God will listen and do our bidding.

Fasting must forever center on Christ. It must be Christ-initiated and scripture-ordained. Like the prophetess Anna, we need to be *worshiping and fasting* (Luke 2:37). Christ points the way. After his baptism, he fasted for forty days, preparing to make his appearance to the public so that he might begin his ministry. He made a specific point, when his disciples could not heal a suffering child: *This kind* [of demon] *never comes out except by prayer and fasting* (Matt 17:21). His message is evident: Fasting and prayer go hand in hand.

Fasting provides wonderful benefits for those who wish to be spiritual people. It is a reminder that when we walk in the path of Christ, we are transformed in his image. If we are tempted to feel anger, bitterness, conflict, fear, depression, jealousy, judgmental—if these negatives nag our minds—a period of reasonable fasting will strengthen our spirit to combat them effectively. Two things happen as we fast. First, we feel hunger pangs and discomfort, a gurgling stomach. We begin to crave food, available or even unavailable. Our stomachs have been trained through years of conditioning to give signals of hunger at certain times. In many ways the stomach is like a spoiled child, and a spoiled child does not need indulgence; it needs discipline. We must not give in to its demands. We can ignore the signals; we can tell our spoiled child to calm down, and before long the pangs should pass. If not, take a sip of water and the stomach will be satisfied. We have to be the master of our stomach, not its slave. In our physical hunger we discover that we can be truly independent of hunger, and we can transform it into a source of spiritual power to prevail over it. This is the ideal time for meditation and prayer. Also, we can invest a few seconds to remind ourselves of the millions whose lives are an everyday fast—not by choice. One may say, *What am I supposed to do? Feed the starving millions?* No, but the thought of them might motivate you to provide aid, according to your ability. It may help to be mindful of the needs of others. Helping the poor and homeless would, no doubt, enhance our fasting exercise.

Second, our fasting leads us toward a spiritual direction. It is not simply food from which we abstain. We withdraw from worldly involvements, enticements, and cravings. Fasting is a serious catharsis of the mind. As we cleanse our bodies for appearance and health reasons, it is imperative to refrain from evil thoughts, lustful desires, sexual fantasies, greed, hate, and revenge. We would feel a sense of relief if we loosened every knot of iniquity, tore up every unrighteous bond, and rid ourselves of unjust accusations against our neighbors. It is the only way to increase the grace of God and maintain peace in our souls. Fasting is of great emotional benefit in our daily life when we fast from corrupting snares, from harmful passions, from the distorted pleasures of the flesh—these are stumbling blocks in our way to peaceful living.

If we are to benefit our health, it is common knowledge that we must be discerning and self-disciplined about what and how much we eat. In our times, special diets and sophisticated programs about dieting have become big business. Many people, influenced by clever advertising, spend hundreds of dollars to engage in a diet program. The objective is to lose weight. If the program works and is needed, it may be the way to go. However, wise teachers from the beginning of written history have propagated the concept of fasting as a spiritual exercise of testing and temperance to refine one's character and to restore one's ailing soul. When we are mentally or physically troubled, we can be sure that our soul is suffering and needs healing. History has recorded many devout people who lived to the great age of 125 years or more; they attribute this to their faith in fasting and prayer.

Fasting enlightens the mind, strengthens the spirit, controls emotions, and tames the passions. Listen to a voice of the fourth century. St. John Chrysostom, a dedicated church father, admonishes:

> When you fast, give proof of it by your behavior. If you see a poor man or woman, take pity on them. Help them as best as you can, according to your own abilities and capabilities. If you see an enemy, be reconciled with him. If you see a friend gaining honor, do not be jealous, rejoice with him. If you see a beautiful or seductive woman, pass her by and keep walking. Let

your eyes fast, teach them not to fix themselves lustily on beautiful faces, or to be allured by strange spectacles. For looking is the food of the eyes, but if it be such as is unlawful or forbidden, looking cunningly mars the fast and upsets the whole safety of the soul. And let the ear fast by refusing to receive evil messages, calumnies, gossip, and false reports. Let the mouth also fast from accusations, judgments, disgraceful stories and slander. For what does it profit if we abstain from dairy products, meat, fish and foul and yet bite and devour other people's personalities. Let your hands fast by being pure from plundering and avarice. Let your feet fast by ceasing from running to immoral shows. Finally, let your whole body observe the fast, and fix three precepts in your mind so that you may accomplish them during fast: to speak ill of no one, to hold no one your enemy, and to expel from your mouth altogether the evil habit of swearing. As the harvester in the fields comes to the end of his labors little by little, so we too must make this rule for ourselves and in any manner come to a consistent practice of these three precepts during fasting. It is the way to arrive to the summing of spiritual wisdom. Then we shall reap the harvest of a favorable hope in this life, and in the life to come we shall stand before Christ with great confidence and enjoy those indescribable blessings of which, God grant, we may all be found worthy to receive through the grace and love of Jesus Christ our Lord. Amen.

Fasting reminds us of Christ who fasted in the desert forty days and forty nights,

> *...and when He was famished, the tempter came and said to Him, "If you are the Son of God, command these stones to become loaves of bread." But He answered, "It is written, 'One does not live by bread alone, but by every word that comes from the mouth of God.'"* (Matt 4:2–5)

Words that come from the mouth of God are recorded in the holy scriptures. It is not food alone that we need; we also need to open our Bibles and nurture our souls with God's word.

It is significant that Satan came to Jesus while he was fasting. Does Satan not also come to us as we fast? Even if we fast minimally, it needs to be in secret. We should not reveal what kind of fasting we are doing, nor should we be curious or judgmental about the quality of fasting of others. Those who desire spiritual blessings should perform their good deeds in secret. They are not to brag about their goodness. Instead, they should pray in the depths of their hearts. God knows our intentions and sees all that is done in secret, and he will reward us for abstinence with abundant grace.

After Christ had spent several hours at the well in Samaria, the disciples, presuming that their master would be starving, brought him lunch. He declared, *I have food to eat of which you do not know....My food is to do the will of my Father who sent me, and to accomplish His work* (John 4:32,34). This was not a clever metaphor but a genuine message of reality. Christ was being nourished and sustained by the power of God. That is the reason for his counsel in Matthew 6. We are told that when we are fasting, we should not act miserably. In essence, we are feeding on God and, just like the Israelites who were sustained in the wilderness by the miraculous manna from heaven, so we are sustained by the word of God. It is available to us as we turn the pages of the Bible.

At times we may be tempted to do or say something that we might later regret. Our human cravings and desires are like rivers that tend to overflow their banks; fasting helps keep them in their proper channels. Fasting is a tool of self-discipline. Pull away from the impending temptation for a few minutes. Think of Christ and his presence in your life. If you feel that your thoughts are demonic, say, *Get behind me Satan*, and move on to do something of spiritual value to you or do something good for someone else. We crave things we do not need, and if we acquire them, we can become enslaved by them. St. Paul writes, *All things are lawful to me, but I will not be enslaved by anything* (1 Cor 6:12).

The disciples of Christ connected their fasting with prayer. They did not separate their fasting from the faith and good works that they offered in obedience to their Lord's life. His commands of compassion, mercy, and love were part of their fasting. Our challenge is to emulate the disciples who maintained a life of prayer and fasting. Fasting is an essential element of our spiritual life that frees us from passion, enables us to gain dominion over our lives, and enables the Holy Spirit who dwells within us to make us instruments of God's will.

Fasting is not at all an act of mortification of the senses for mortification's sake. It is not *a little suffering* that is somehow pleasing to God. It is not *a punishment* that is to be sorrowfully endured as payment for sins. It is not given to us in the context of *law*, which, if endured, would gain us favor in the sight of God, and, if ignored, would denounce us as sinful and guilty. As people of God, we are called upon to fast joyfully, knowing that the aim of fasting is not the fasting itself but rather the giving of permission to the Holy Spirit to direct our lives and to prepare us for the celebration of a holy day.

Thoughts to Consider:

- Fasting must be done for the glory of God and as an expression of honoring Christ, our eyes singly fixed on him. Our intention should be to worship and glorify our Heavenly Father for all the blessings that he bestows upon us daily.

- Fasting and prayer should be intricately bound together. True fasting begins by being in charge of our thoughts, casting off evil, bridling the tongue, cutting off anger, and controlling lust, evil talking, lies, and cursing. The cessation of these is the beginning of a true fast.

- A brief period of fast can be a joyful experience. It is not so much an abstinence from food as it is a feasting on the word of God. Food does not sustain us. It is God who sustains us in all things—when we are connected with him in prayer, as we obey and apply his teachings, and as we walk the path of Christ with honesty, humility, and love.

Chapter 15

The Art of Praying

When you pray, you must not be like the hypocrites;
for they love to stand and pray in the synagogues and
in the street corners, that they may be seen by
people...but go into your room, shut the door and
pray to your Father in secret...and in praying, do not
heap up empty phrases as the Gentiles do, thinking
that they will be heard for their many words.

Matthew 6:5–9

The essential element of prayer is believing that God is an ever-present reality. He is the caring Father who is attentive to our thoughts, our actions, our needs, and our well-being. He is the Creator and Sustainer of the Universe and of all life. Prayer is what keeps us connected with him. Each prayer we offer reacquaints us with God's purpose in our life. Regular prayer is a source of strength that we derive from the Almighty God, which makes our life possible. Our physical self, besides healthy nutrition, needs oxygen to survive. Our spiritual self, our soul, requires prayer for its nourishment and sustenance.

The above scriptural verse lays the foundation for the *art of prayer*. Mainly, prayer is an intimate and private issue, which needs to be said in a simple way, in few words, and with a large dose of humility. Being omniscient and ever-present, God knows exactly what is in our heart. In Luke 18:9–14, we find two men in prayer—a Pharisee and a tax collector. The Pharisee by himself, proudly standing before God at the altar, enumerates his virtues of obedience and generosity. The tax collector, regretful for his sinful actions, stands far off; he does not even look up to heaven, but in groaning humility, prays, *God, be merciful to me, a sinner.* In the eyes of God, the sinner finds justice because of his humility. The message of the story is evident: Our prayers need to avoid the high-flown speech of the Pharisee, who was bursting with pride, bragging about his righteousness and worthiness in comparison with others. It is easy to understand why the tax collector's attitude of humility was rewarded.

As we explore the whole concept of prayer, we discover that it is essentially a state of standing before God. It is turning the mind and heart toward our Creator. To pray means to stand before God—body, soul, and mind, mentally to gaze unswervingly at him and to converse with him with respect and hope. This state of *standing before God* may be accompanied by words, or it may be silent: Sometimes we speak to God, sometimes we simply remain in his presence, saying nothing, but aware that he is near us, closer to us than our own soul. Theophan the recluse puts it:

> *Inner prayer means heart and mind together standing before God, either simply living in His presence, or expressing supplication, thanksgiving, and glorification.*

In *The Art of Prayer,* Theophan describes three elements in a human being—body, soul, and spirit. The body is made of earth; yet it is not something dead but alive and endowed with a living soul. Into this soul is breathed a spirit—the spirit of God, intended to help us to know God, to reverence him, to seek and taste him, and to have joy in him. The soul, then, is the basic principle of life—it is what makes a human being something alive, as opposed to an inanimate mass of flesh. While the soul exists primarily on the natural plane, the spirit brings us into contact with the order of divine realities. The spirit is the highest faculty of a human being, that which enables us to enter into communion with God. As such, man's spirit—with a small *s*—is closely linked with the Third Person of the Trinity, the Holy Spirit of God—with a capital S; although connected, the two are not identical—to confuse them would be to end in pantheism.

Body, soul, and spirit—each has its special way of knowing: the body, through the five senses; the soul, through intellectual reasoning; the spirit, through the conscience, through a mystical perception that transcends ordinary human processes. Just as there are three elements in a human being, so there are three main degrees of prayer:

1. **Oral or bodily prayer:** This is a prayer of the lips and tongue. The prayer consists of reading or reciting certain words or making requests, while kneeling or standing. It is essential not to ramble on endlessly and use inconsistent phrases, but to concentrate inwardly on the meaning of what we say, to confine our mind within the words of the prayer.

2. **Prayer of the mind:** As we pray orally, we gradually notice that the mind prays the words inwardly without any move-

ment of the lips. Sometimes the mind prays without form-
ing any words at all. As we advance in the ways of prayer, it
is still reasonable to use ordinary oral prayer, because oral
prayer is at the same time an inner prayer of the mind.

3. **Prayer of the heart:** Oral or mental, prayer is still incom-
plete. It is necessary for it to descend from head to heart—
to find the place of the heart, to bring down the mind into
the heart, and in a state of inner peace to unite the mind
with the heart. Then prayer will become truly *prayer of the
heart*—a prayer not of one faculty alone, but of the whole
human being, soul, spirit, and body. Effective prayer is not
a result of our intelligence or of our natural reason, but of
the spirit with its special power of direct contact with God.

When the three aspects of a prayer are in harmony, the
praying person experiences certain feelings that enrich prayer.
For example, as we start our prayers, we may feel sensitive, a
sweet soreness of the heart, which indicates a feeling of repentance for some of the wrongdoings in our life. As we continue
our prayer, the feelings of human unworthiness and regret
become a sentiment of warm tenderness, which, in essence, is a
response to God's acceptance and love. Most important of all is
the sense of spiritual warmth—the flame of God's grace warming our hearts, accepting us, forgiving us, and loving us. In time
of prayer we can truly envision ourselves enveloped in a radiant
cloud of grace, in the presence of our Lord, symbolically entering the mystery of the transfiguration on Mount Tabor (Mark
9:2–8). As we look at him with the eyes of faith, we draw from

this vision the sweetness of spiritual joy. We look to Jesus the pioneer and perfecter of our faith.

Prayer is the unique channel of communication through which we become more conscious of God. Through prayer we learn of God's great love for us, and we find comfort, peace, and joy in his presence. From age to age in every land and culture, human beings reach out through various means to connect with their Creator. Something in the human heart yearns to understand the origins of the universe, the beginning of life.

In our high-tech times, as we employ the latest electronic devices to communicate with the world around us—and we do this remarkably well—the spirit within us emerges and yearns for what is more, for what is better, beautiful, real, and lasting. Made as we are in the image and likeness of God, our hearts cannot rest until they rest in him.

Prayer is a human journey back to God. It is a personal journey we take in time among our fellow travelers, but it is also a timeless journey we take alone toward eternity. Through prayer, we discern the truth of our own spiritual identity, the inseparable relationship of God and his people. Through prayer we connect with the ultimate reality, God, and discover who we are in his creation. A spiritual understanding of him transforms our frowns into smiles, gives us a sense of belonging—we are his people and he is our Father. He gives us life, heals the sick and afflicted, and reforms the sinner.

Our Lord Jesus Christ urges us to watch and pray—that is, always be alert and keep in touch with God, the source of life. He emphasized the need for persistence in prayer. *Seek, and you shall find…knock, and it shall be opened to you. For everyone who asks receives; and the one who seeks finds; and to him that knocks it shall be opened.*

When we pray for things that are good and beneficial to our spiritual life, our prayers are answered. God knows the difference between wants and needs far better than we do. What we truly need, we will have, and prayer based on spiritual understanding will help us become more conscious of the good that is already ours and at hand. Sometimes, however, we need to be persistent in our prayer before we can see it clearly.

The measure of all prayer is inner harmony. When we free ourselves from physical limitations and materialistic needs, we become more aware of our spiritual identity. Then we know that we are ready to pray correctly and effectively. If, on the other hand, wants and human desires still seem to elude us, we should not give up. A deeper understanding of our true being as a spiritual entity is on the way! In the meantime, we must know that God loves us, wants us, and takes care of us. We need to strengthen our faith in God's goodness and his wish for us to have joy and peace.

We need to think of prayer as a joyous experience in our daily life. It is not a labor to be performed. It is a way of celebrating our unique and special meeting with the Creator. It is an intimate journey. As we pray, Christ becomes our companion in everyday life, protecting, enlightening, strengthening us.

As his people, we must pray personally and privately or as Christ taught us, in secret. If we pray only in the public worship of the church, even there, sometimes our prayer becomes a shallow and superficial experience. As we pray alone, behind closed doors, not merely in our rooms but in the room of our hearts, we experience that special intimacy. Then, our dialogue becomes real. We reveal our innermost secrets, requests, needs, problems. We can ask God for anything. Nothing is too small or too insignificant. But we must ask with faith, possessing the conviction that God does hear our prayers and he does answer in the way known only to himself. Sometimes we are impatient and we want God to answer immediately; that's our human nature. Like children, we demand things. But God has his own plans for us and takes his time to respond. If our prayers go unanswered, it does not mean that God ignores our requests. God's delay is not denial. God gives us a chance to think about what we are asking and to be absolutely sure that our requests are beneficial to our lives.

The following prayer merits our attention:

I asked God for strength, that I might achieve,
I was made weak, that I might learn humbly to obey.

I asked for health, that I might do greater things,
I was given infirmity, that I might do better things.

I asked for riches, that I might be happy,
I was given poverty that I might be wise.

I asked for power that I might have the praise of men,
I was given weakness, that I might feel the need of
*   God.*

I asked for all things, that I might enjoy life,
I was given life, that I might enjoy all things.

*I got nothing that I asked for—but everything I had
    hoped for.*
*Almost despite myself, my unspoken prayers were
    answered.*

I am, among all men, most richly blessed.
    (Anonymous)

There may be a time in our life when our prayers may go unanswered. Ardently we pray and pray, make offerings, go to our church in full anticipation that our wish will be granted— and nothing happens. Understandably, we feel disappointed. Sometimes, we may even doubt that God really hears our prayers.

True, we may not receive the desired, specific response to our prayers. Is God acting cruelly? No, but it may be that God is warming up our prayers and hugging us tightly to prepare us for service and life ahead. After all, God's ultimate desire is to draw you and me into a relationship with him. Created to act in freedom and return God's love to others, we have a purpose beyond the present moment. What seems our immediate need may be a result of anxiety but not good for us. God knows exactly the yearnings of our hearts and may have something different and better in mind for us. We need to trust his unconditional love.

Confronted by the futility of our prayers, we may feel like giving up on divine providence, thinking that God does not care. Or we may start rationalizing or blaming ourselves: *I don't have enough faith. Maybe God is punishing me for something bad I've done. I guess I'm not worthy.*

This type of thinking indicates that our image of God is not accurate. We may be projecting our own perceptions. No matter what happens, God is on our side when we pray, and prayer is an act of love. We cannot manipulate God's response to our prayers. He loves us and knows what is best for us. We have to accept God's answer—one that always, though sometimes mysteriously, represents the fullest measure of his love.

In prayer, God is present to us in curious ways. We may not know he is there except by the evidence afterward. In our time of need, when we are desperate, God may seem silent, absent, or distant. Through the gift of time, however, it is often possible to look back and discover that God was there all along—sustaining, comforting, encouraging. We may recall previous times of trial and pain when God did **not fail** us.

In our human condition, we may be angry with God because he did not grant our wish. *Why God? Why me? I'm a good person!* When we allow ourselves to express such passion—to demand an answer to our *whys?*—is to take God seriously, to enter the intimacy into which God invites us, and to acknowledge God's providential power and care.

My Aunt Helen, afflicted with unbearable, excruciating pain in both knees, an incurable arthritic condition, kept arguing with God: *I have been a person of prayer all my life. Charity was my secret mission. Why are you causing me all this pain? What wrong have I done?* I could not convince her that God did not cause her condition. When I assured her that God did not enjoy human suffering but, rather, gives us the strength to endure it, she reacted with a smile and said, *I guess I cannot blame God for my salt addiction.* Then she went on to admit that since an early age and all her life she consumed a lot of salt.

To argue with God may be a compliment. Obviously, being human, we doubt that he is there for us. But once we have expressed and processed our frustration, it is then time to let go and let God take over. Holding on to our angry feelings will only disturb our life and cause alienation. However, saying, *Let your will be done in my life* is more promising. Why? Because we are in very good company.

Joseph Elijah, a non-Christian whose emotional turmoil turned into long-term physical pain, read about the tragedy of Christ on the hill of Golgotha and wrote:

> *This evening I, too, come to You, sweet Brother of Nazareth,*
> *Drowning within me barbaric passions and wild hate,*
> *To cry in front of the blood-stained body of the most beautiful soul*
> *That has ever brought flowers of love in this wretched world.*
>
> *O modest Lily of Galilee, in front of Your resplendent light,*
> *How many times have the hopes of the humble fluttered!*
> *A number of crosses were erected across Your own.*
> *Alas, to the crucifiers! Most of them were Your own people,*

You are not the first, nor will You be the last to be cru-
cified,
Sweet Jesus, in this world of bitterness and malice.
However, Your glory is immaculate among the genera-
tion of mortals:
Whether You are or are not the Son of God,
You are the God of suffering who understands my
pain.

Although our anguish makes us feel alone and lonely, we are in a blessed company. Jesus Christ is present in our life — our prayer is an intimate journey with him. Furthermore, in our Bible reading, we will discover personalities who deal with the silence of God. The most famous is Job, a devout and just man, who did not blame God for his misfortunes, even when he lost his family and properties. Remember, Jesus' agonizing prayer in the garden of Gethsemane: *Father, remove this cup* [the crucifixion] *from me,* was not answered.

Throughout human history, countless cries of need and hope have sought God's ear. A few have claimed responses of miracles. Many have received favorable answers. Most, perhaps, have experienced the mystery of ambiguity that calls for reflection and faith.

Patience and persistence in prayer are imperative, in spite of the realization that God's plan of response involves our ultimate salvation. If a loving father answered all the demands of his child, he might be supplying his little one with destructive components. A wise parent establishes boundaries, gives what seems to be for the good of the child's wellness and holds back what is bad. Our Heavenly Father hears our needs. He remains loving. Being all-wise, he knows what to allow that is of benefit to the soul and what is not. The best gift he can give us or the best solution to our problems is the divine one. The specific answer that we wish to our prayer—though a good and worthy one—may obstruct God's ultimate, eternal design and purpose. Even so, God is at our side as a co-sufferer, longing to comfort us and feeling our pain as only an infinite lover can. The most effective prayer we can offer is the one that seeks to make our will conform to God's will, to make our way of thinking run parallel to God's way of thinking. Prayer, as our expression of love and trust, symbolizes this relationship between God and us.

Thoughts to Consider:

- As you are about to pray, take a minute to examine your perceptions of God. Is he a benevolent Father, dispenser of rewards for good behavior? Is your image of God one of a rigid parent, a dutiful judge who dispenses punishment for wrong behavior?

- Imagine what your life would be like if God granted answers to all your prayers, especially the demanding ones. If your prayers remain unanswered, can you endure the agony of waiting? Better yet, can you change your style of prayer, emulating Jesus in the garden of Gethsemane whose agonizing prayer ended, *Not my will, let Your will be done.*

- If you are disappointed with God's delay, can you in your prayers revise the image that you have of God? Can you see him as the Bible portrays him—a walking companion, intimate friend, loving father, comforting mother, anxious parent, passionate debater, and co-sufferer in the hours of your personal pain?

The Ultimate Reality

As your real self surfaces unencumbered by negative influences, you feel responsive to and responsible for your choices. You will interact with others with self-confidence and in full awareness that God's invisible presence is with you. You will treat others with compassion and understanding. Clean and refined, comforted by God's ocean of mercy and forgiveness, your soul will empower your every step. Adversities will be less intimidating. You will face evil with spiritual temerity, because in the process of theosis—deification—you will not feel alone. Our loving God and Creator will be at your side, sustaining and directing your life.

Chapter 16

Combating Resistances

Many men and women attained glory and real joy by surrendering themselves in complete submission to the will of God, employing no reluctance or resistance to Him, as a violin surrenders itself to the complete will of a fine musician.

Kahlil Gibran

Obstacles are part of life—visible most of the time—and can be prudently encountered. Carefully overcoming one obstacle at a time, we experience inner joy, renewed strength, and feel invigorated. Resistances are more subtle than obstacles and tend to be invisible. We have good intentions of doing something worthwhile, and for some unknown reason we fail to act. Sometimes the stronger and more common resistances surface from within, causing lack of energy to prevent us from carrying out our good intention. We become passive; we do not want to have responsibilities; we avoid using our God-given properties even for our own good; and we suffer emotional and spiritual deterioration. St. Paul experienced the inner warfare, which he describes briefly in his epistle to the Romans.

I see another law in parts of my body warring against the law of my mind, making me captive to the law of sin that dwells in me. I do not understand my own actions. For I do not do what I want, but I do the very thing I hate. Wretched man that I am! Who will rescue me from this body of death? (Rom 7:23–24)

At other times, resistances appear with a smile, tempting us with sweet talk, or they come to us in the form of advice or place us in a provocative situation. For example, if we try to do something for the benefit of ourselves or for someone else or for an organization, in the process we can be sure unexpected resistances will surface from somewhere. A relative or friend, individuals that we probably know and respect, will say, *That's not a good thing to do. It's a waste of your time.*

I recall a personal experience. My family and I decided to go to Africa as missionaries to help out the indigenous in some capacity. As we made plans, half a dozen well-meaning friends presented us with reasons not to take such a risk: *It's dangerous. You could get sick. There's an AIDS epidemic. Civil war is raging; you could get shot. Why do you want to go to Africa anyway? There are plenty of people here who need care. I think you are not making a wise decision.*

Did my thoughts waver? Yes! I began to doubt the purpose of our involvement. Maybe we could offer help in our immediate environment; that certainly would be less taxing. My thoughts became negative. However, my belief in the familiar axiom, *Where there's a will there's a way,* came to my assistance. When we truly make up our minds to do something worthwhile, we move into action in spite of the risks.

My wife, my daughter, and I did go to Africa for a whole month. We cherish this experience and are grateful for the enrichment it brought to our lives. We witnessed poverty, hunger, illness, unsanitary home conditions, lack of medical care, and no clean water. At the same time we discovered undaunted spirits, warm and receptive hearts, kindness, hospitality, and strong faith in God. In spite of our exposure to the dangers of that mission, all went well with us. We received more than we were able to give to the people; we were impressed by their gratitude for what is available to them, and their appreciation for life, simple as it was. They did not have much in the way of material possessions, but they did have spiritual wealth. In spite of their poverty-stricken appearance and living conditions, joyfully they attended church services, clapping their hands and singing praises to God. They participated physically with body movements and spiritually with stentorian voices. An invigorating and invincible spirit permeated their gatherings; they were amazing and energetic with a zeal that nurtured a life of contentment and faith.

As we climb the spiritual ladder, trying to live in agreement with God's will, we encounter aspects of life that are difficult and, at times, insurmountable. Opposing forces from without and from within hinder our ascent. We agonize. To comfort ourselves, restlessly we wander and seek new attractions. We busy ourselves in self-gratification; we seek ongoing entertainment. Strange voices clutter our minds, preventing us from listening to the voice of our own soul which assures that we are capable of doing the right thing in the eyes of God and for our own benefit.

A major resistance in pursuing a spiritual life is the fear of death. It affects everyone by its very existence, and we are devastated when it touches a loved one. When we experience the tragedy of death through the loss of a child, a spouse, a sibling, or a dear friend, we feel the impact of helplessness and succumb to despair. Both birth and death are mysteries. What truly happens to us after we die is the great unknown. Chapter 10 provides convincing evidence that evokes comforting answers.

It is impossible in any spiritual endeavor to bypass or ignore the needs either of our physical self or the complexities of human existence. Sometimes we delay, avoid, or ignore a good deed that we want to do, and, at times, to please others, we conform and do deeds that tend to damage our personal integrity or stifle our spiritual growth. When the current is against us, we tend to blame other things and other people; we may even think that God does not want us to be happy here on Earth, that he allows misery and suffering in this life, as the price of happiness in the life to come. This is totally wrong and possibly was perceived by the punitive or guilty minds of those who projected their own perceptions of God.

As we consider the benefits of fasting or praying—as delineated in the previous two chapters—some inner forces provide reasons that render us unable to pursue the possibility of such benefits. We feel weak if we abstain from our regular diet; we find reasons to prove to ourselves that fasting is of no value. Ironically, countless people spend enormous amounts of money on diet and physical fitness programs, believing in the slim and beautiful bony creatures they see advertised on television. Why not see fasting as a form of spiritual exercise that benefits our physical health and nurtures our spirit?

Prayer is a good habit to develop in our daily life, we say to ourselves, and we may pray regularly for a while, but gradually we drift away from the practice. In any beneficial endeavor, the *drifting away* is a phenomenon that is common among humans. We justify it by saying to ourselves that we are either too tired or too busy. If we begin with the premise that *the spirit is willing but the flesh is weak* and accept that as a reality, then we can continue our spiritual ascent fully aware of our resistances. Spirituality is strengthened by our knowledge that we are children of God, living in harmony with our inner wisdom, our soul, and coming to a full sense of gratitude for the miracle we call life. God wants us to be happy right here on Earth, and prayer points out the way. Momentarily, we need to close our eyes and open our hearts, and our inner perceptions will discover the truth of life and the purpose of our existence. All things are God's creation and are perceived by our minds. The world is ours to cherish and share. If our physical self did not get hungry or thirsty, we would not look for water, food, and nourishment. If our hearts did not have a longing for affection and love, we would not look for someone to love and someone to love us. If we were not spiritual beings, we would not question God's presence and the purpose of our lives.

As our emotions demonstrate themselves through bodily reactions of anger, anxiety, frustration, fear, indifference, pain, and sorrow, why not recognize them as our own resistances? We do not have to express these feelings at random or defend them to prove a point. At best, we can recognize them, accept and be in charge of them, use them wisely and try to climb higher. *Avoid an hour of anger to live a hundred years,* claims an old proverb. Of course, monitoring and being in charge of any emotions requires effort.

It is generally thought that good things are accomplished through hard work. St. Gregory of Sinai was of the same opinion: *No work...which lacks pain and effort ever produces fruit.* In order to see results of our efforts, we need to observe how we individually approach everyday life. This entails being aware of who we are; in spite of our fragile self—body, soul, and mind—we must focus on priorities, a lifestyle that takes into consideration God's presence and providence in his creation, nature, and people.

Although we may have studied carefully all the contents of the first four steps of this book, we may still not be totally aware of how God is an intimate companion of our life's journey, how he is active in our daily existence. As we study each phase, he facilitates our ascent by placing our resistances in perspective and by opening our hearts to make us more receptive to his messages.

God wants to be more and more in our lives, and it is truly our choice to expand our awareness of his presence or to exclude him. He is not just a superpower abiding in heaven and controlling the universe. He is also in our soul, and. therefore, our attempt must be to contact, penetrate, and connect with our soul, the spiritual part of our humanity. What abides in the world of our soul is not something subjective, human creation; it is something objective, something *placed* there by another, the living God himself, the Creator who breathed life into the dust, placing there his own image and likeness. He is the Creator and makes us creators. His likeness is Spiritual and makes us spiritual.

During the last fifty years, philosophical, psychological, and secular ideologies focused on humanistic approaches to living. Many people, in their search for a better life, embraced certain ideals and values, such as becoming aware and more conscious of human existence, but in the process they left God out or ignored his part in the creation and sustenance of the world. The idea that happiness lies in getting what we want when we want it—satisfying our instinctive appetites and desires—proved to be futile. Reality points out that even if we could satisfy our every desire and fulfill every dream, we would not be satisfied. Exclusive self-gratification, far from making us happy, makes us greedy and miserable. Do you recall the myth of King Midas and the Golden Touch? It is time for those who have been victimized by the humanistic approach—exclusively trying to appease the drive of false ego—to consider a more rewarding approach to life, a spiritual one.

How do we start? Initially, we invite God into our lives. God is the provider and sustainer of our existence. He brought us thus far and has provided us with perfect means to eliminate the misery of our wrong perceptions and to free us from the slavery of materialism and insatiable desires. The model is ever-present. It is the flawless personality of our Lord Jesus Christ and our guide is his gospel. If we do not have a legible copy of his teachings, can we buy a Bible and take it home? As we start reading the story of Christ's appearance on Earth, what he did for the world and asked us to do for our own wellness, instantly we discover God's infinite love and wisdom. He knows what is best for us. He loves us unconditionally and wants us to live a good and joyful life, to be generous and share whatever good we enjoy. In spite of our weaknesses, lack of faith, and loss of hope, and all the wrongs that exist in our world, we could choose to accept his all-embracing invitation: Come to Me all of you that labor and are heavily burdened, and I shall give you rest.

There is nothing wrong with becoming aware and increasing our consciousness. These are pivotal points for they reassure us of our inner need, a spiritual function that is an activity of the soul. Through *increased consciousness* we are attempting to develop a relationship with our inner self, our soul, as a way of reaching out and touching the life of another person, who also is a son or a daughter of God. Deep down in our hearts, most of us know what godly behavior is, and yet we postpone action. Must we wait for a crisis, or illness, or approaching death in order to develop a spiritual life?

When we combat resistances, which could be our own personal shortcomings, life may become more difficult before it becomes more coherent and tranquil. A great deal depends on what aspect of life we have been ignoring. A major part of spirituality is concerned with qualities of our human spirit—such as love, compassion, contentment, forgiveness, a sense of responsibility, a need for harmony—that bring happiness to both self and others.

When we make an effort to be compassionate, forgiving, loving, patient, and tolerant people, we will recognize to some extent the potential impact of our attitude toward others and how much our modeling influences and shapes their conduct. As we interact with others and notice certain negative forces surfacing, we get to know and understand ourselves a lot better. Our patience and perseverance to be kind and tolerant can be most rewarding. Patience strengthens the spirit, sweetens the temper, stifles anger, bridles the tongue, restrains the hand, and tramples on temptations. Impatience takes away the joy of being alive.

An immature person reacts aggressively to a negative situation or a problem. A mature person waits patiently, evaluates the situation wisely, and moves on to a viable resolution with confidence. A spiritual person recognizes his or her limited reasoning and ability and turns to God for guidance. Individuals who turn to God's word discover key principles to become people of patience and emotional stability. Patience, persistence, and prayer are assets to our spiritual growth, revealing our levels of faith in times of stress and difficulty. Faith is a yearning within us that seeks to connect with the ultimate power, God. When we feel anxious or pressured over a dilemma, although we want an immediate answer, it is to our benefit to wait. As difficult as this waiting may seem, it is a cooling-off period when synergy becomes reality. God is at work with our soul, coordinating and directing our efforts to our well-being. It is time to see the truth about ourselves and the reality of our situation.

Attaining spirituality totally alone, excluding family members and immediate others, serves no purpose. Without being aloof or pompous, we could be models of Christian behavior. We do not have to be a light that will illuminate the whole city, but we could be a candle that lights up the darkness of someone's world. We never know the hour or the moment when we touch someone's life without even being aware. When we begin to see others as children of God, with a soul and needs similar to ours, we may recognize the spark of divinity in them. This is not an emotional, psychological, physical, or metaphysical experience. It is a major purpose of our existence—to connect with our soul, relate with other people, and treat them not as functions but as brothers and sisters, and as we interact with them, we clearly seek communion with God.

Our Lord offers a tangible example of what communion with God truly means: *I am the vine, you are the branches.*

The vine branches cannot exist without the vine, their source of life. God is the vine and we are the branches. We cannot possibly exist and bear fruit without being connected with the vine. When we distance ourselves from God, we become animallike and rebel against the limits of our nature. We desire other limits, and we do not know what it would mean to satisfy this greed. We make ourselves addicted to pleasure, pursuing areas of self-satisfaction at any cost. As a result, we lose sight of *moderation in everything.* We become miserable and resort to artificial means to regain happiness. Is that really the way we want to go?

Thoughts to Consider:

- To develop a spiritual life may be difficult, but it remains the only road to inner joy, serenity, and peace in this life, on this planet. Once you start your spiritual journey, the Holy Spirit becomes your companion, to guide you, to strengthen you, and make the way smoother.

- Place yourself in God's hands as soon as you wake up in the morning. Recite the Lord's Prayer slowly. When you get to the words, *Thy will be done,* pause for a moment and think of a way to do God's will. Then, throughout the day, be aware of his will as it is made known to you through your attitude as you interact with other people at home, at work, and at social functions.

- Start each day with the Serenity Prayer:

  *God, grant me the **serenity** to accept the things I cannot change, **courage** to change the things I can, and **wisdom** to know the difference—living one day at a time; enjoying one hour at a time; accepting hardships without complaints.*

  This world as it is, may not be as you would like. Christ admonishes that we can be in this world but we don't have to be of this world. Simply, you do not have to conform to the world's style of life.

Chapter 17

Refining the Soul

*If you forgive men their trespasses, your Heavenly
Father will also forgive you. But if you do not forgive
others, neither will your Father forgive your trespasses.*
Matthew 6:14–15

Spirituality is a process of becoming, moving through various levels from low to high, climbing over obstacles, and transcending resistances. A major principle to be learned is forgiveness. Without forgiveness spiritual life is unattainable. It is necessary, for a few precious moments, to consider the concept of forgiveness. How else can we continue our inner journey if we do not unload our burdens, wrongs we have done in life or wrongs and injustices done to us?

The true meaning of the word *forgive* is *to let go*, and that is the best we can expect. If we let go, it does not mean that we resign from life and living. It means that the outcome is no longer in our hands. If we let go of the hurt, it does not mean that we deny reality around us. It means that we have no choice but to endure the pain as real and allow healing to take over every hour of the day. Christ, the physician of bodies and souls, is ever available. Trust him. This very moment, he is closer to us than we are to a loved one who is holding our hand. He is eager and ready to accept us, to forgive us, to cure our ailments and loneliness, because he loves us unconditionally. This does not suggest that God approves our wrongful actions.

If hurt is part of life—and at one time or another we all get hurt—we need to find a way to heal. Otherwise, unhealed hurts linger on, damaging our existence and causing more pain. Think of the wrongs done to us as snake bites. There are two sources of pain: One is the bite itself, the visible wound, which cannot be undone—it bleeds or hurts, and we can see the wound where the fangs penetrated the flesh. The second source of pain is the venom that circulates in our blood—it is the killer. No one has ever died of a snake bite; it is the aftershock of the venom permeating the body that can be fatal in certain cases. The venom is the killer, not the bite. A similar situation occurs with hatred and the desire to seek revenge. Although the wound has externally healed, the unforgiving attitude continues to poison our inner world. We have the choice and the power to extract the killer poison of unforgiveness.

Next to love and acceptance, forgiveness is one of the most important ingredients in our lives. Remember: *To err is human; to forgive is divine.* Nothing is more powerful in our relationships than the realization that, as imperfect humans, we all make mistakes. Relationships consist of humans, and no human is ever an angel. Apart from our unwitting errors, knowingly and often without legitimate reason we cause each other to suffer. We lie, we break promises, humiliate each other, use abusive and violent language, neglect and ignore the other, betray significant others, pummel and abandon each other. We often do these things, not to our enemies but to the people closest to us, precipitating serious pain in intimate relationships, husbands and wives, children and parents, and friends. These emotional injuries are often left unresolved and festering, causing not only ill feelings but physical ailments.

Think about your own experience for a moment. Think back to the last time someone really hurt you or wronged you or took something that belonged to you, whether a possession or an opportunity. Besides instant anger, did you feel like retaliating? Did you feel like fighting for your rights? These are normal reactions to being hurt or being taking advantage of. Take another moment and think what your reaction does to you on the emotional as well as on the physical level. Improper response to your injury automatically impairs your own health. You have no joy or peace when someone injures you. Probably you want to strike back, get revenge, get even. Rarely would you consider responding gently to an individual who injured you, and rarely would you seek reconciliation. Pain and anger prevent you from being understanding, patient, or kind to a person who has wronged you. Your hurtful attitude filters into other relationships that otherwise might be rewarding. People sense that something is wrong with you and either avoid you or maintain their distance. As a result, you feel alienated, angry, confused, disturbed, embittered, and passive, and you do not really know how to regain peace.

Have you ever been hurt? Were you abused as a child? Were you sexually molested? Did you feel neglected or rejected by your parents? Did one or both of your parents like one of your siblings more than they liked you? When you were a child, did you suffer through your parents' marriage or divorce? Were you coerced into pursuing a career different from the one you wanted? Did the mate of your dreams betray you for the love of another?

If you answer *yes* to any of the above questions, you may be on the brink of being set free from a suffocating bondage that you did not know was keeping you a victim. Your hurts are not precious artifacts that must be displayed in your living room; whatever happened in your past could make you sick or cause you to be a loser. You do not have to be a loser, and do not, for a moment, think that you are a victim. You are neither a victim nor a loser. You are about to invite into your life what has always been the only remedy for the healing and recovery of broken hearts.

You need to practice the art of forgiveness. Most of the wounds that you have suffered are not unforgivable. You can put them behind you and go on with your life. You must learn to forgive and let go of those who have hurt you, so that you may regain inner peace.

This arduous journey involves a struggle against anything that degrades or distorts the beauty of soul, body, and mind. An unforgiving attitude stifles the potential of the soul. God reveals himself to the pure in soul: *Blessed are the pure in heart, for they shall see God* (Matt 5:8). It is purity of heart and soul that enables us to draw near to God. Our soul may need serious and sensitive surgery to remove lingering blemishes and distortions of attitude. God will perform this spiritual surgery, because he wants to remove the bitterness and the hurt. It may hurt a bit, but it will surely heal. We need not be afraid, for the one who *cleanses every stain*, the Holy Spirit, is ever present to assist the process of our recovery. All we need to do is cooperate.

The practical, visible effects of communion with God are seen in our daily behavior, character, and relationships. Our life as a whole is seen to be shaped by the habitual practice of

Christ's teachings. From this comes stability, vitality, a steady
and consistent life, and a ready will to obey Christ rather than to
deny his love. These spiritual fruits bear witness that Christ truly
lives within a person. *I live, yet not I, but Christ lives in me*, the
apostle Paul reassures us. As we walk step by step with him, we
soon discover that no desire can be fully satisfied when it is outside of God. As we come into the joyful presence of God, getting
our own way loses its meaning. The only thing we have to do is
be attentive to his presence at every moment. While we pay
attention to his presence, welling up in our heart come whispers
of divine guidance and love that make life radiant.

Those of us who are serious about obeying and following
the spiritual way set down by Christ have certainly been troubled
by the words: *Forgive us our debts as we have forgiven our debtors.*
It is not always too happy a thought to be told, in the Lord's
Prayer, that we must give in order to receive; that we must let
loose and let go of all indignation, no matter how justified it may
be. Even the apostle Peter asked, *Master, how often shall we forgive; until seven times?* Jesus answered, *I say to you, until seventy
times seven.* In his abundant love, our Lord said *seventy times
seven* to reassure us that his forgiveness is immeasurable.
Regardless of how many times we fail or do the wrong thing, his
mercy and love are available to us. All we need to do is to repent,
change our mind about harmful behavior, and return to him
with an honest determination to follow his teachings.

While on the cross, suffering an agonizing death, Jesus
said, *Father, forgive them,* [let them go], *for they do not know
what they do* (Luke 23:34). His gentle voice from the hill of
Golgotha reaches our ears today, instructing us to forgive those

who have hurt us, to let go of the grudges and ill feelings that we hold against them. Of course we need to be forgiven, but we also need to forgive others.

Peter could well have been saying, *You just can't go on forgiving people! Just how much can a person take?* But Jesus put it on the basis of law, rather than emotion. If we want light in the room, we must flick the switch. If we refuse, we will sit in the darkness—and the darkness is of our own choosing. We may feel that it is too much to forgive those who have deliberately and spitefully used us; that we have the right to our indignation and bitterness. But we will have to pay the price for a broken connection in the divine plan. We may choose unforgiveness, and thus we are choosing discomfort and, perhaps, even ulcers, heart trouble, and misfortunes in every area of our life. The answer is: Switch on the light. Let go of bitterness, not so much because our *enemy* deserves or does not deserve to be forgiven or because the mistake against us is justified, but because *we* need to forgive. We need the healing of our soul, and that can be accomplished only by right thinking.

How can we approach God if we carry the burden of anger, jealousy, or malice against anyone? We need to hear the words of the apostle James, *Draw near to God and He will draw near to you. Cleanse your hands, you sinners, and purify your hearts* (Jas 4:8). We must learn to forgive and forget the offenses of others and realize that true forgiveness flows only from a strength and purity of soul. Christ spoke to the heart of the matter when he said:

> *When you are about to offer your gift at the altar, and suddenly you remember that your brother or sister has*

something against you, leave your gift there before the altar and go; first be reconciled to your brother or sister, and then come and offer your gift. (Matt 5:23–25)

Reconciliation, kindness, sympathetic understanding, charity, and love–these are attributes that prepare the way for forgiveness. However far along the path toward spirituality we may have traveled, we still make mistakes. As long as we acknowledge our shortcomings, weaknesses, and sins, there will arise the necessity to be forgiven for the faults, flaws, and offenses that characterize our thoughts and actions. As long as we have a need to be forgiven, we must pardon others for their trespasses. It takes an open mind and a gentle heart to view the situation through another's eyes, to get his or her outlook, perspective, and viewpoint. It is easy to criticize, judge, condemn another person. Our Lord reminds us of our eagerness to judge others: *Why do you see the speck in your neighbor's eye but do not notice the log in your own eye?* People who hate and seek revenge are ever ready to justify their attitude. As a result, they blind their soul to the good that exists in another human being. Revenge is a boomerang that harms the person who hurls invective more than it hurts the victim. The person who is not content until he gets even with the aggressor holds himself on a low plane, bringing darkness to his soul, confusion to his mind, and illness or even death to his body.

We have a striking example of compassion in Victor Hugo's classic novel, *Les Miserables*, when the old bishop touches the soul of a thief. The central theme interwoven in the story is the power of loving forgiveness and expiation on the one hand, and the complete inability to forgive, compelled by hate-driven vengeance, on the other. The two characters are Jean Valjean, a petty thief who spends nineteen years in prison for stealing a loaf of bread and then finds himself an outcast in the outside world, and his nemesis, the relentless Javert, a police inspector who is obsessed with law and order.

Valjean leaves prison only to commit another crime, robbing silverware from a kindly bishop who had befriended him. Caught by the police, he is brought back to the bishop to return the stolen silverware. Looking compassionately at the thief, the bishop refuses to acknowledge that a crime has been committed. *I forgot to give you these*, says the bishop, handing the thief two expensive silver candlesticks to add to the contents of his pack. As well as giving the generous gifts, the bishop offers a flash of illumination: gently, he urges the man, whose sentence has already been served, to learn from that suffering instead of resenting it. *If you are leaving your sad past in the prison with hatred and anger against men, you deserve compassion; if you leave it with good will, gentleness, and peace, you are better than any of us.* The bishop's act of forgiveness transforms the outcast Valjean into a new man. Haunted forever by the bishop's actions, Valjean moves on with his new life, a forgiving man, kind to other offenders, and generous.

At the other pole stands Javert, totally unable to forgive or forget, pursuing Valjean mechanically, allowing neither head nor heart to interfere with his perverse sense of duty and retribution. Fanatically obsessed by respect for authority and hatred for rebellion, Javert, as a self-appointed prosecutor of the law, is determined to extract retribution from the man who escaped prison. During the revolution when Javert is captured and about to be executed by his opponents, Valjean is the one who bravely intervenes and rescues him. Javert cannot believe it. His unforgiving mind wonders, *How can I allow this man to hold dominion over me? This desperate man that I have hunted gave me my life. He gave me my freedom.* Feeling empty and useless, he could not tolerate Valjean's act of compassion. *I want to escape from the world of Jean Valjean. There is nowhere I can turn; there is no way to go on.* He plunges into the river and drowns. Blinded by his unforgiving spirit, he destroys himself.

When human beings lived in ignorance of their relationship with one another, an eye for an eye and a tooth for a tooth was the prevailing attitude toward the wrongdoer. As people became more civilized and more aware of the human condition, they gradually realized the wisdom taught by Christ: *If a man shall strike you on one cheek, turn the other.* Turning the other cheek implies *love that endures all things.* Striking back implies hatred. As we turn the other cheek, it means that we move away from the evil and look in the direction of the Holy Spirit who is the comforter. We invite him to enter our lives and cleanse our stains.

Spirituality seeks that we treat ourselves and others as Christ would treat us—with the spirit of acceptance, compassion, and forgiveness. When people behave unlovingly—yelling, cheating, lying, stealing, killing—they have lost touch with their divine essence, their soul. They have forgotten who they are, God's children. Could their evil behavior be a cry for acceptance and love? If we are to continue walking in a spiritual path, we have to take conscious responsibility for what we choose to perceive—the guilt of our brothers or sisters that we need to judge and punish, or their probable innocence that could be encouraged. We would be pleasantly surprised to see the unusual, if we treated people with compassion and forgiveness. They would be less likely to respond defensively and would probably be more open to repentance and correction.

Few of us can capture the exuberant spirit of forgiveness and its true application better than a village priest called Papavasile, whose legendary story is recorded in the private archives of the church. His experience is so moving it can hardly be described within a few paragraphs:

On a Friday evening during Lent after World War II, Papavasile was hearing confessions. His parishioners, young and old, waited in line for their turn.

Twenty-six-year-old Dimitri, serving his second year as church cantor, was the last in line to confess. Six months before, he had been engaged to the priest's daughter, Sophia. [In the Greek Orthodox tradition, priests are allowed to get married and have families.] As he began to confess, Dimitri burst into uncontrollable tears. Papavasile, sensing the inner turmoil of his future son-in-law, placed an empathic arm on his shoulder, and said, "Dimitri, whatever is in your heart let it out. Christ is a loving and compassionate God. His mercy is immeasurable."

"I have killed a young man," Dimitri said, still sobbing. He went on to acknowledge that one dark night, thinking that the young man was one of the Nazi soldiers who had burned his town and killed his parents, he attacked him. Between painful sighs and tears, Dimitri confessed that not only had he jumped from behind and choked the young man to death, he had then removed the chain and cross from his neck.

Shocked at Dimitri's crime, the priest took the cross in his hand. To his horror, the priest realized it was the very cross he had given to his son Christos as a graduation present. At long last, the unresolved mystery of his son's death was revealed. Now came the dilemma. As a priest, Papavasile was commissioned to pronounce forgiveness. Should he allow the murderer of his son to marry his daughter? The priest gazed momentarily at the crucifix behind the altar, sighed deeply, and thought: *If he can forgive all sins, who am I to deny forgiveness to a penitent soul?* On the one hand, he was the father of the murdered son and of the soon-to-be-married daughter, and on the other hand, he was a priest in God's service. Papavasile forgave Dimitri and allowed him to marry his daughter.

Did this priest have angry feelings, rage, hatred? As a normal human being, of course he did. But he also had compassion, facing a man in true repentance. God's grace accomplishes what may seem to be impossible to our human minds. The Holy Spirit enabled Papavasile to transcend human emotions and to act divinely. Did his pain stop? Did the memory of his son's unjust death fade away? Probably not. But as he walked step by step in the presence of God, he found comfort by extending unconditional love toward his future son-in-law, Dimitri.

Your sins are forgiven you, are the words of Jesus that Dimitri absorbed, and he responded with gratitude. Liberated from the burden of guilt, Dimitri had to learn how to let go of the self-condemnation that could bring more pain and suffering than any outside destructive force. He accepted God's gift of forgiveness and made a new life for himself; he became a devout member of his faith, a loyal citizen, and a good family man. In order to gain freedom from the relentless pressure of self-condemnation, we must learn to forgive ourselves and to forgive others.

Often we refuse self-forgiveness because we are disappointed in ourselves. *How could I have done such a thing?* Through self-judgment and self-condemnation we choose a form of self-centered behavior and end up blocking God's abundant love and forgiveness. If we persist in not forgiving ourselves, we negate God's love for us, ignoring his forgiveness and building up a reserve of stagnant guilt. We become emotionally and spiritually numb, even depressed, and controlled by these worthless feelings. The source of many emotional conflicts is the refusal to forgive one's self. Self-forgiveness does not mean absolving ourselves of the responsibilities and consequences of our actions, but rather it emphasizes them all the more. It does not mean self-pity, but accountability and repentance and change. It does not mean whitewashing or condoning our violations, but facing the harsh reality of our actions and picking up our cross and following Jesus.

Forgiveness is a process that can be painful and, at times, unending. Whatever our pain, whatever our situation, we cannot afford to hold on to an unforgiving spirit another day. Think for a moment: Someone hurt us or violated our private life in some way. We are angry, we feel victimized, and we do not want to see or forgive that person. We might even plan to retaliate. But the question is: *Who is suffering more, the violator or the victim?* It seems that victims suffer more because they nurture angry feelings. When we feel betrayed by someone, instead of sulking, clinging to pain and resentment, we can use this time to strengthen soul and body by practicing *letting go*. An effort to forgive the one who has hurt us may change our direction in life. Change implies spiritual growth.

During our brief stay here on earth, why should we indulge in hating anyone? Let us rather exchange good deeds for evil ones, forgiving an offender; by doing so we contact his soul and lead him toward the light. If we continuously emphasize the good in a person, the positive forces will soon predominate. They will then assume command of the soul, liberating it from the fetters of the evil forces that have held it in bondage, ignorance, and darkness.

Here we are faced with a challenge: When we get involved in the process of forgiving others, we will discover what it means to be free-spirited people. As we persist and keep our eyes on Christ who forgave us and continues to forgive us, it will be a liberating force like nothing else we have ever experienced. The apostle Paul admonishes, *Be kind to one another, tender-hearted, forgiving each other, as God in Christ also has forgiven you* (Eph 4:32). To make God's gift of forgiveness our own practice, we must develop our faith in Christ. Then, we can trust him to apply his work of grace and reconciliation.

Thoughts to Consider:

- Forgiveness is the act of setting someone free from an obligation to you that is the result of a wrong done to you. Forgiveness, then, involves three elements: injury, a debt resulting from the injury, and a cancellation of the debt. All three elements are essential if forgiveness is to take place.

- To experience the joy of forgiveness, you may need a change of heart, and that comes with *metanoia.* — the word derives from the verb *metanoo,* meaning *I change my mind, I repent.* Once you feel regret for whatever wrong you have done, and you are willing to follow a new direction, the grace of forgiveness will fill your heart with peace and joy.

- Forgiveness is liberating, but it is also sometimes painful. It is liberating, because you are freed from the heavy burden of guilt, bitterness, and anger that you have harbored within. It is painful because it is difficult to have to face the truth about yourself. You will be able to accept and forgive others, as you allow the Holy Spirit to help you.

Chapter 18

Metanoia — Repentance

O Lifegiver Lord, open the gates of repentance to me.
My spirit since dawn every day gravitates around Your
*   Holy Temple.*
I am bringing to You the temple of my body that is
*   tarnished with sin and infirmities.*
However, being that You are a merciful God, cleanse
*   me through Your compassionate mercy and show*
*   me the way.*

Anonymous

This ancient hymn speaks of the human yearning to come closer to God, yet feeling unworthy. The awareness of sin, which tarnishes soul and body, makes it difficult. However, believing in a merciful God, we realize that he does not want us to perish. He wants us to live a happy and fulfilled life. He is willing to cleanse us from every stain of sin.

As we become aware of our errors, and as we feel inner turmoil, emotional pain, and discomfort, we know it is time to change. The change is critical. It takes time and effort. It may cause pain and tears. Out of pain comes growth, wisdom, and a new direction. When we feel betrayed by someone, instead of sulking, clinging to resentment, and playing the role of victim, we are challenged to strengthen our soul and body through forgiveness. By forgiving the person who hurt us, or asking forgiveness from someone we might have hurt, we are taking a major step toward a spiritual direction. Such a change of mind implies spiritual growth.

Metanoia is derived from the word *metanoo*—meaning *I change my mind, I repent.* A sequel to the above hymn explains the benefits of repentance.

> *As I become aware of the multitude of my errors, my evil deeds, I tremble out of fear, thinking about the terrible Day of Judgment. But trusting the compassion of Your mercy, I appeal to You like David. Have mercy upon me, O God, since You are a merciful God.*

This penitential hymn is a by-product of David's remorseful heart, as described in Psalm 51. David's life was a series of success stories until he reached the age of fifty. Under his rule as king of Israel, his prosperous nation had extended its borders. Then David, the shepherd, young man, musician, soldier, statesman, and monarch committed two great crimes: adultery and murder.

The blackness of his sin and its troublesome consequences to him and to his kingdom make one wonder why David is called the *God-inspired prophet.* As we read his psalms where he expresses his profound sorrow, his change of mind, we appreciate the sincerity of his repentance.

In the Book of Kings, written in later years, we read: *David did that which was right in the eyes of God and obeyed Him all the days of his life. He produced fruits of repentance.* What stands out in David's life is a recognition and acknowledgment of his violations, followed by his desire to change. Read the following psalm that summarizes his state of repentance:

> *Have mercy on me, O God,*
> *in the greatness of Your love;*
> *In the abundance of Your tender mercies,*
> *wipe out my offense.*
>
> *Wash me thoroughly from my iniquity,*
> *and cleanse me from my sin,*
> *For I am well aware of my iniquity,*
> *and my sin is before me always.*
>
> *It is You alone I have offended:*
> *I have done what is evil in Your sight.*
> *Wherefore You are justified in Your charges*
> *and triumphant in Your judgment.*
>
> *Behold, I was born in iniquities,*
> *and in sin my mother conceived me.*
> *But You are the lover of truth,*
> *You have shown the hidden depths of Your wisdom.*
>
> *Sprinkle me with hyssop, and I shall be pure,*
> *cleanse me, and I shall be whiter than snow;*
> *Let me hear sounds of joy and feasting;*
> *the bones that were afflicted shall rejoice.*
>
> *Turn Your face away from my offenses,*
> *and wipe off all my sins,*

A spotless heart create in me, O God!
Renew a steadfast spirit in my breast.

Cast me not away from Your face;
take not Your blessed Spirit out of me;
Restore to me the joy of Your salvation,
and let Your guiding Spirit dwell in me.

I will teach Your ways to the sinner,
and the wicked shall return to You.
Deliver me from blood-guilt, O God, my saving God,
and my tongue will joyfully sing Your justice.

O Lord, You will open my lips
and my mouth shall declare Your praise.
Had I known Your desired sacrifice, I would have offered it,
but You will not be satisfied with whole-burnt offerings.

Sacrifice to God is a contrite spirit,
a crushed and humbled heart God will not spurn,
In Your kindness, O Lord, be bountiful to Zion,
may the walls of Jerusalem be restored.
Then will You delight in proper oblation,
in sacrifice and whole-burnt offerings,
Then shall they offer calves
upon Your altar.

In the Old Testament, Jonah continually preached repentance to the people of Nineveh until they repented. Ezekiel preached repentance:

Therefore, I will judge you, O House of Israel, everyone according to his or her ways, said the Lord. Repent, and turn yourselves from all your transgressions; so iniquity shall not be your ruin. (Ezek 18:30)

The New Testament provides us with a number of stories in which the characters went through a radical transformation. Their names are familiar: Zacchaeus the chief tax collector, the prodigal son, the woman from Samaria, Mary Magdalene, Saul of Tarsus. All were violators of God's law, and they describe eloquently the change that took place within them. *Metanoia*, this inner change, is the turning point in our lives, thoughts, feelings, actions, and attitudes. Our lives take a new direction.

When you feel you are on the right track, there is no reason to change what is already good. Repentance or the change of lifestyle is for those who are aware that something is not quite right. Sometimes we cause our own discomfort. At other times, we subject ourselves to painful experiences or to negative influences, and we suffer the consequences. We may choose to blame others for our condition, but deep down, we know that our failure or our current pain most of the time is the result of our choices.

A spiritual life may be the new path to inner joy and peace. Most churches today, like clinics, provide services, messages of comfort, and a climate of healing. Here, as we experience God's unconditional love and forgiveness, our souls feel nurtured. Emerging from a spiritual experience, we feel fulfilled and empowered to rediscover our purpose in life.

The record of the four gospels shows that Christ's mission started with the preaching of repentance. This change of heart and mind implies an awareness of wrongs and a desire to leave the state of sin behind and forge ahead with courage and faith toward a new life near our Lord Jesus.

Repent, for the Kingdom of heaven is at hand (Matt 4:17). With these words, Christ called upon men and women to acknowledge their sins and return to the Father. God's love and compassion could not be poured upon defiled souls. Real repentance has to take place—not just *I'm sorry I did that*—but a genuine *repentance,* which means *to change attitude; to turn away from; to make amends; to take a new and healthier direction.*

In the New Testament, repentance is mentioned seventy times. Repentance was the poignant call of John the Baptist (Matt 3:2). Apostle Peter's sermon, which motivated three thousand people to be baptized on the Day of Pentecost, stressed repentance:

> *Repent and be baptized every one of you in the name of Jesus Christ, for the remission of your sins.* (Acts 2:38)

Repentance was preached by St. Paul when he was

> *...testifying both to the Jews and to the Greeks, repentance toward God, and faith toward our Lord Jesus Christ.* (Acts 20:21)

When we do something radically wrong, we experience a deep sense of guilt. We want to find a trustworthy confidant to reveal the truth about ourselves. Whether a priest or a minister or a spiritual counselor, the confidant must be a person of faith, humble, godly, nonjudgmental, stable, and positive.

When King David committed adultery and murder, he realized that his sin was not simply against his subjects; it was a sin against God. He felt guilty. In his own words: *Against You, You alone, have I sinned, and done what is evil in Your sight* (Ps 5:5).

Guilt is a feeling that results from either self-judgment or the judgment of others. Whether we sin against ourselves or against other people, the guilt is toward God. True guilt is that which results from divine judgment. In other words, we sense that, in the eyes of God, we did something wrong. His wish is that we live a life of righteousness before him, so that he can bless us fully with every good thing. He has planned and prepared for us. What is our part? Since we have a loving God who created us after his image and has given us a beautiful world to live in and enjoy, at least we need to be on good terms with him.

Normal people would like to get rid of their guilty feelings, for guilt is an evil force, an insidious feeling that initially causes passivity and gradually psychosomatic illness. Guilt causes anxiety, emotional pain, and fear. In extreme cases, it results in violent behavior, even suicide. God does not want us to feel guilty. He instills in us the desire to seek forgiveness and restoration of the suffering self.

People who want to straighten their lives, to restore a positive sense of self, may seek to atone for the wrong they have done. This sense of atonement is a healthy moral desire to restore themselves to their former condition, freed from their guilt, to a state of joyful living. It is remarkable how deep-seated this desire is, and how long-lived it can be. If guilt and atonement run parallel to each other, we may assume that even a tinge of guilt can be our first step toward penance, regret over the wrongs, and eventually confession.

Thoughts to Consider:

- As you begin a new life and slowly ascend the spiritual ladder that brings you into your soul, pressures of outward events will no longer distract you. On the contrary, you will be able to control and combat any adverse influence with the guidance of the Holy Spirit.

- You are no longer alone. Your cleansed heart becomes the throne where the Holy Spirit sits as a king and ordains how things should be directed and carried out. This inner kingdom begins from the first moment of inner transformation and entrance of grace, but initially it is not experienced to its fullest perfection.

- Gradually, you will receive the invisible strength of the Holy Spirit to rule over all your inner and outer life, according to God's good will and pleasure. It is then that the kingdom of God awakens within and begins to manifest its natural power.

Chapter 19

Confession — A Choice

> *Confess your sins to each other and pray for each*
> *other so that you may be healed. The earnest prayer of*
> *a righteous person has great power and wonderful*
> *results.*
>
> James 5:16

We have often heard people saying, *I have a confession to make*. It gives them a moment of relief before their speech. In essence, they are acknowledging that they did or said something wrong. The Greek word for confess, *exomologo*, comes from *exo*, meaning *I bring out*; *omo*, meaning *what is in me*; and *logo*, meaning *verbalize*. *Confess* implies disclosing or acknowledging something damaging or discomforting to oneself. It also means the revealing of one's sins to God, to a priest, to a minister of the church, or to a spiritual counselor. Confession is the act of admitting and divulging guilt in the hope of regaining relief and peace of mind.

When we make a personal confession, it presupposes that we have become aware of wrongs committed; we have feelings of regret and repentance, and we desire to realign ourselves and walk with God. A major problem that many face is the inability to comprehend the mercy and love of God. Because we have a hard time forgiving others, we project this attribute of *unforgiv-*

ing spirit to God. Haunted by our sins and unable to let go of our past life, we say, *Oh, God will never forgive me.*

We tend to make up God's mind, not considering the truth that we have a loving God who does not punish. As soon as we realize and regret the wrong we have committed, he forgives us. The discomfort and punishment that we sense are not imposed by God. They are consequences of our negative attitude and wrong actions. Through his prophet Isaiah, God says, *I, I am He who blots out your transgressions for my own sake, and I will not remember your sins* (Isa 43:25).

It is natural for a normal human being to share a joyful or sorrowful event with a sympathetic person who listens attentively and in a nonjudgmental way. The joy is doubled and the sorrow is shared. In emotional issues, a spiritual person is usually a good listener as well as a great comforter and advisor.

It is sad that countless people turn to the occult to provide comfort for themselves. Even some churchgoing people consult mediums, card or palm-readers, hoping to gain insight to face their problems. They believe that knowledge of the future, through visits to fortune-tellers, readers of tea leaves and tarot cards, will give them wisdom to manipulate and control the future. They do not realize that, in their search for the truth, they are turning to those who are in league with the father of lies: the devil himself! Why would anyone ignore a trusted treasury of countless blessings that Christ makes available though his teachings and seek solace from a convicted liar?

People who put their trust in fortune-tellers—thinking of them as gifted persons with special powers—are actually putting their trust in the devil and encouraging a contact with the enemy of the soul. That type of a relationship can be unsettling and ultimately destructive.

No person knows fully what is best for us, what is right for us, or what God has planned for our benefit. God alone knows—not a guru, not a teacher, not a mentor, not even a parent or a friend. Only God knows what our future will be. A seasoned and wise priest, minister, or spiritual counselor may help us discern God's plan and possibly point out options for a new direction. Such a person who attentively listens to our confession may help us to see aspects of ourselves and become aware of our potential. That is a far cry from dictating our future or saying with certainty, *This is what is going to happen.* Only God knows with certainty what tomorrow holds for us and the rest of the world. God created you and me in his image; we have a free will to decide our actions and responses in life.

When we sit in a draft, we may catch a cold, and sickness is our penalty for violating a natural law. When people violate a traffic law, they either cause an accident or they pay a fine for the violation. The accident or the fine is the penalty. No matter what law we violate, we are accountable, and usually undesirable consequences follow. When we violate God's law, initially our penalty is a guilty conscience and remorse. When we commit a crime or a sin—disobeying the will of God—we experience a gnawing remorse, and we no longer feel at peace. Our mental state suffers; we feel unhappy, anxious, and depressed, and sometimes these emotional issues cause physical ailments. Psychotherapy, once reserved for special cases, is now in vogue for the masses. Many people resort to therapists to relieve themselves from the wrongs in their life.

With the exception of severe psychological problems that require psychiatric intervention, most people with disturbing feelings of sin and guilt find relief and healing by going to confession and seeking reconciliation with God. Repentance precipitates a desire to restore any possible damage and seek a healthier way of life. To pave the way at this point, we can make a clear distinction between a sin and a mistake.

Briefly stated, a sin is a choice to do something that we know is against God's will. A sin is a willful act—one that is calculated, thought out, anticipated, and performed when fully conscious. A sin is deliberate. Seldom will one commit a sin by mere accident. A mistake is usually made on the spur of the moment; it is unplanned and made without forethought of consequences. A mistake is a miscalculation, common to all humans, an error in judgment—frequently based on an error in research or information received. We can turn to God directly and ask him to convert our mistakes and errors, the stumbling stones in our life, into stepping stones. Each mistake contains a lesson. When we are dealing with our violations, wrongs, and transgressions, we need God's intervention.

When the wrong is confessed, the sense of guilt is washed away, and peace of mind and soul returns. In my twenty-two years of ministry in the church and thirty years in the healing arts as a psychotherapist, I have seen many tormented souls in sheer agony: guilt and regret, undermined mental and physical health. After a few minutes of true confession, a wonderful change, a transformation took place. Smiles of relief, peace, relaxation, and a new attitude replaced the previous condition of the repentant. Gratefully, they left my office with new hope and courage.

Someone may say, *Nonsense! All illusion. All emotional deception. All magic. All self-hypnosis.* That may be the perception of an agnostic or a disbeliever. I shall listen to such comments when the particular methods of hypnosis or magic used by these critics bring about similar results. I do not claim personal power or skills that helped the penitents who came to me. I served only as a humble instrument of God's grace. My part in their confession was to listen with empathy and to counsel the suffering soul with respect and sensitivity, in full awareness of the human condition. That is the part that the penitent soul finds of great comfort and healing.

As we sharpen our focus on the true concept of confession, we realize that it is an experience of atonement, removal of guilt, and gradual personal transformation. It needs to be done in the presence of a pious and prudent listener, one who can listen to our confession with concern and empathy. Such a person can be truly an instrument in the hands of God for our spiritual direction. The gentle advice and reflection that we receive help us to see our real self, control our passions, or at least lessen the presence of evil in our lives.

The urge to confess wrongdoings is deep. We know and believe that God will forgive us, or, at best, he has already forgiven us, since we have turned to him with a repentant heart. Sin stimulates remorse and shame in the individual who believes in the principles of the Christian faith. These feelings, known as guilt, lead to that state of mind called penitence. A penitent needs to be reassured of God's mercy and his forgiveness. This may sound like a matter of emotions only; however, the Christian community throughout history has always recognized

the significance of emotions. Penitence and the search for forgiveness are not simply duties owed to an injured friend or to
God. They are emotional necessities securing hope and freedom
of action toward a healthier future.

Believers who are trying to walk in the path of truth and
righteousness often find opposing forces. The fact that there is
sin constitutes a conflict within. *Sin is always in front of me*, King
David complained. The tempter will attempt to lure us against
the will of God: *It's just a small sin; not a big deal; everybody does
it. We are only human; we still sin. We don't want to, but we still
do. Even Paul the apostle admitted: I do what I don't want to do,
and I don't do what I want to do* (Rom 7:19).

The moment we sense that we have violated the law of
God, we can pause and pray:

> *Dear Lord, our merciful Father, I am struggling to live
> a good life. I am not doing well; I am failing. I am
> angry with myself. I am frustrated. No one really
> understands what I am facing. Please forgive me and
> direct my steps back to your will. Help me to believe
> and accept the fact that You are a loving and forgiving
> God. You proved that to me on the cross two thousand
> years ago, yet I am haunted by doubt. I need Your sup-
> port and guidance. Amen.*

There is a desire to acknowledge one's guilt, but the deeper
and more insistent desire of the penitent is to be reassured of
God's forgiveness. This is another reason why confession contributes immensely toward the restoration of our inner fragmen-

tation. What the Roman Catholic and the Greek Orthodox churches offer through the holy sacrament of confession, and what the Protestant world makes available through the art of pastoral counseling are valuable elements for a sound spiritual life. The individual pours out his or her soul and receives relief and worthwhile advice. The confessing person feels better and conceivably finds a new direction in life. This is a reality that cannot be ignored.

Confession needs to be accompanied by absolution, total and absolute forgiveness. By the power that our Lord Jesus Christ has left with his church to absolve all sinners who truly repent and believe in him, the one who hears the confession, acting in Christ's name, absolves the penitent from sin, conveying complete forgiveness. This is part of the healing ministry of the church, reassuring us that our God is a God of love and mercy. All we need to do is take that initial step.

At one time or another you may have shared with a friend an unbearable secret that haunted you. Didn't that sharing relieve you considerably? You felt lighter and probably happier because you had a much needed friend and sympathetic ear to listen to what was troubling you. Some people find psychotherapy of great therapeutic value. Why? Because someone trained to listen empathetically is there for them. Psychologists of distinction have come to recognize clearly and with increasing appreciation the wholesome and healing influence that confession exercises upon the mental health of people who find in it relief and encouragement.

If the mere telling of a failure or a mistake to a sympathetic friend affords us consolation and relief, in the eyes of God genuine confession will give us greater and more beneficial results. God's pardon restores and strengthens peace and tranquility to a troubled soul. It is always available. The question is: *Are we available to God?*

Thoughts to Consider:

- When you are wrestling with evil thoughts or behavior and you sense the weight of guilt, it is possible that you have been subjected to temptation or negative thinking. Now is the time to take a good inventory and make amends. There is hope.

- Accept the potential of a spiritual life. Our Lord waits for your return to his flock, a better life for you, and a life of grace and reconciliation. His very presence will free you, empower you, and cause you to change to a person who is cleansed, pure, holy, good, and productive.

- Find a confidant who will be available to you as a spiritual companion in your new journey through life; choose one who reflects your faith and confidence in Christ.

Chapter 20

Theosis — Deification

*When Christianity speaks of the imitation of God, it
means imitating **Christ** because He is God incarnate.
Christians emulate the thoughts of Christ, desires,
intentions, virtues. They are also inspired by the saints
because such persons were particularly expert at
Christ-imitation and, therefore, at God imitation.*

Jeffrey K. Salkin

The word *theosis* derives from the Greek word for God,
Theos. Therefore, *theosis* means *deification* or *becoming divine.*
This process penetrates our humanity and restores it to its original state, just as God created humans in the beginning. In this
way, we participate in the creative energy of God. As we transcend our own being, negative notions or distorted perceptions
about life, we become fully human and more Godlike, the way
God would like us to be.

Most Christians have known that the way to get closer to
God is to try to become — feelings, thoughts and actions — *like*
God. Psychologist Erich Fromm said, *Man is not God, nor
could he become God. He can become **like** God.* Being like
God is the twin notion that we are created in God's image.
God is holy. You shall be holy, for I, the Eternal God, am holy
(Lev 19:1).

When Moses asked to see God's face, God refused his request since *no one can see Me and live.* Instead, God told Moses about his divine essence:

> *Compassionate and gracious, slow to anger, abounding in love and faithfulness, extending kindness to the thousandth generation, meaning for ever, forgiving iniquity, transgression, and sin.* (Exod 34:6)

On one occasion, the disciples said to Jesus, *Teacher, show us the Father.*

Jesus replied, *No one has ever seen God except the one who came down from heaven*—meaning himself. Further, he added, *Anyone who has seen Me has seen the Father.*

Our finite eyes cannot see God, yet our faith propels us to perceive and accept his attributes and be *like* God. Being that God is gracious and compassionate, we must be gracious and compassionate. Being that God is beneficent, we must be beneficent. Being that God is loving, we must be loving.

Our *theosis*—deification—becomes a reality as we study the gospels. There, with the eyes of faith and a receptive heart, we encounter God in human form, Jesus Christ, whom we want to imitate. Visualizing his appearance and life on earth, reading of his healing through touch, and hearing his teachings, we experience the ceaseless pulse of divine love as it moves endlessly from the Father to the Son to the Holy Spirit. We have a chance to participate in the work of the Holy Spirit whose purpose is to deify us, to make us temples of God's presence.

The incarnation of Christ bridges the gap between God and the world, opening the way to *theosis*. Jesus put on humanity so that we might put on divinity—*Christ in you, the hope of glory*, says Paul the apostle. The incarnation occurred in order to open the possibility of *theosis*, our sanctification. God became man not only because of original sin. He became man so that man might become God. The incarnation of Christ is not simply a way of undoing the effects of original sin, but it is an essential stage of our human journey from the divine image to the divine likeness. In becoming man, Christ empowered us to share in his own divine nature. God the Father sent the Holy Spirit into our hearts to fill us ever more and more with divine life and power.

Theosis then results from the incarnation, which includes the crucifixion, resurrection, pentecost, and ascension. Through the incarnation, human nature was renewed and restored in Christ and made us capable of participating in the life of the Trinity, a life of harmony and creativity. Paul Evdokimov writes,

> *The profound reason for the Incarnation does not come from man, but from God, from His desire to become Man and to make of humanity a Theophany, the beloved ground of His glorious Presence.*

In his epistles, the apostle Paul urges his followers to acquire the mind of Christ (1 Cor 2:16), and the heart of Christ (Eph 3:17) that they may fulfill their destiny, according to God's will, to be what God wants them to be. Paul is not advocating an external imitation or a simple ethical improvement but a real

Christification. His life is a true example of *theosis*, as he claims, *I live, yet not I, but Christ lives in me* (Gal 2:20).

Bishop Kallistos Ware defines *theosis* as *Christification*, implying a way of being *like* Christ:

> We are called to attain the likeness of Christ. It is through Jesus Christ the God-man that we are divinized, made "sharers of the divine nature." (2 Pet 1:4)
>
> By assuming our humanity, Christ who is the Son of God by nature has made us sons and daughters of God by grace and love.

As we get deeper into our hearts and become aware of our human condition, we may wish to change certain aspects that are undesirable. We have no reliable source but God to whom we turn in fervent prayer for his mercy. The power of prayer is remarkable. It is a firm ladder that joins heaven and earth. We need to climb this spiritual ladder to unite with God whose energies will be available to us. Through prayer, simple human beings become illumined by the light of the Holy Spirit; they experience an inner serenity, and they walk in the Lord's presence, and discover the priceless steps to becoming more like Christ daily. However, along with our prayers for his help, we must overcome obstacles that oppose God's grace if we wish to use his energies and powers in our lives.

We may ask: How will it benefit us? Through these energies, we enter into healthier relationships with people. We see others as God sees them, sons and daughters, potential members of his kingdom. Love is poured into our hearts through the Holy

Spirit (Rom 5:5). It is only through the practice of this unselfish love, an energy that comes to us from God, that we are in communion with God himself and in communion with our brothers and sisters. It is through the practice of genuine love that we achieve the purpose of our creation: salvation and *theosis*.

Once we begin to feel and experience the rewards of a spiritual life, the true Christian living, we realize the purpose of *theosis*. Its goal is to proceed from the restored *image* of God to the *likeness* of God. The likeness of God is not given to us at random. Through God's grace, we have to make a concerted effort to attain it, pursuing our own spiritual life.

In reference to the image and likeness of God in a human being, Bishop Maximos Aghiorgoussis states:

> *Image is the potential given to humans, through which to obtain the life of Theosis (communion with God). Likeness with God is the actualization of this potential; it is becoming more and more what one already is; becoming God's image and more God-like.*

Gregory of Nyssa (330–395), a man who maintained a life of intimacy with God, speaks of the image of God in human beings with great faith and confidence:

> *For this is the safest way to protect the good things you enjoy, by realizing how much your Creator has honored you above all other creatures. He did not make the heavens in His image, nor the moon, nor the sun, nor the beauty of the stars, not anything else which surpasses all understanding. You alone are a similitude of*

Eternal Beauty, and if you look at Him, you will become what He is, imitating Him who shines within you, whose glory is reflected in your purity. Nothing in all creation can equal your grandeur. All the heavens can fit in the palm of God's hand...and though He is so great...you can wholly embrace Him. He dwells within you...He pervades your entire being.

As we read over the above lines and meditate on Gregory's words, we lay a solid foundation for our personal *theosis*.

Theosis is not only what will happen to us in life after death, when our earthly bodies will be changed into heavenly bodies at the resurrection (1 Cor 15:5–55). It is also God's gracious gift of a new and abundant life here and now, as we experience the mystery of the living Christ through faith, prayer, and charity work. This is not a pious fantasy, convincing ourselves that we are God's people, because we believe, pray, and go to church. *Theosis* is a reality that beneficially and generously we share as we interact with other people in a Christlike manner.

Participating in God's energies implies that each of us interweaves Christian virtues in our relationships. Deified, being Christlike, we emulate his spirit of compassion, justice, love, and understanding. Christ complements our interactions with others, when he says:

Come, O blessed of my Father, inherit the kingdom prepared for you...for I was hungry and you gave me food, I was thirsty and you gave me drink, I was a stranger and you welcomed me, I was naked and you clothed me, I was sick and you visited me, I was in prison and you came to me. Truly, I say to you, as you did it to one of the least of my brethren, you did it to Me. (Matt 25:34–40)

Christ's expectation of us is clearly defined. If we want to be members of God's kingdom, we must enter our suffering society and do the work that he did: feed the hungry, quench the thirst of those in need, extend hospitality, clothe the naked, visit the ones who are sick and those who are in prison. Simply, do not be totally absorbed with yourselves; be mindful of the needs of others.

Basil the Great (330–379), bishop of Caesarea (now central Turkey), in emulating Christ's earthly mission, invested a lifetime giving aid to the poor and sick. He built the first hospital in church history, which was erected in the form of a cross, and he appropriated his wealth to build a complex of charity institutions known as *Vasilias*, for the needs of his flock. His caring spirit is preserved partially in a fragment of a prayer:

According to the abundance of Your love, have mercy upon these people; maintain their marriage-bond in peace and harmony; nurture the infants; guide the young; embrace the aged; encourage the faint-hearted. Gather the scattered, and turn them from their wandering astray. Liberate those who are tormented by unclean spirits; be a companion to those who travel; safeguard the widows; protect the orphans; free the captives; heal the sick. Be ever mindful, O God, of those

*who are under trial, and in prison, and in bitter labors,
and in all affliction, distress and tribulation. Pour out
upon them Your rich mercy. Lord our God, You know
the name and the age of every human being, even from
their mothers' womb. For you are the Helper of the
helpless, the Hope of the hopeless, the Savior of the
storm-tossed, the Haven of the voyager, the Healer of
the sick. You are all things to young and old, the only
One who knows the needs of all people.*

Church history has recorded the lives of many people who
were Christlike, such as Basil the Great; included in the list are
men and women who radiated grace, generosity, humility, and
love. They were not converted once. They were not *born again*
just once. Nor did they repent just once. Every day they sinned
and every day they repented. Repentance and conversion were
their daily challenges. Their lives were a constant care for the
well-being of others. Theirs was the goal of high calling in Jesus
Christ. This is *theosis*.

As we express admiration for the highest human accomplishments in our times, we should not overlook a basic endow-
ment that has occurred since the beginning of creation: God
called all humans to become gods by grace. *I say, you are gods*,
said Jesus, quoting Psalm 82:6 and John 10:34. The word *gods*,
which Jesus quoted, was applied to people. It speaks of the God-
given potential of *theosis*. John Chrysostom writes:

*I said you are gods and all of you are sons and daugh-
ters of the Most High. And this is said because you*

have been born of God. How and in what manner? Through the washing of regeneration and renewal in the Holy Spirit.

Human beings contain God in themselves, united with him inseparably, having the potential of growing into the stature of the Son of God. We are called to *grow up in Him in all things,* the apostle Paul tells us (Eph 4:15). Our destiny is the highest of all human goals: *We shall be like him.* To see Christ face to face, to be with him in intimate fellowship, to be like him—this is the goal of spiritual life: this is the destiny of every Christian soul. The true greatness of humanity lies in God's esteem of a human being, wanting each of us to be like his Son. This is *theosis.*

Theosis is truly a beautiful belief and wonderful state of being, but what does it say to those who are suffering from a terminal illness? How does it apply to people who have suddenly lost a loved one? What does it say to a couple who cannot restore a troublesome marriage? How does it help a man or woman who, with all good intentions, would like to marry but cannot find a suitable mate? What does it say to a person who is laid off from work after twenty years of faithful service and has been unemployed for the last six months? How does it apply to a widow who has lost her only son? What sort of comfort does it offer to men and women in the armed forces on the brink of war? For all these questions that we honestly ask, rational answers are not sufficient. The answers that we need to have can only come from a divine source. How could that be if we detach ourselves from God? We have time for everything else that we need and want. What about time with God?

We work very hard. Most people do. Professionals work an average of fifty-two hours a week; college-educated workers in their thirties and forties work even longer. The amount of time we spend at work has been steadily rising for the last seventy years. Demands and pressures of life require hard work to meet expenses, and status comes at a high price. One does not have to be a radical to note that there are some major shortcomings in the capitalistic system we have created. We sense that we have become spiritually damaged by the pernicious cycle of working/wanting/having as ends in themselves. What happens to family when a home becomes a motel to sleep in between business trips? What happens to stability when mobility is the price of advancement? What happens to meaning and purpose when much of life is a blur?

The lawyer who asked Jesus, *Which is the greatest commandment?* was probably living in a similar blur. Jesus answered

You shall love the Lord your God with all your heart, and with all your soul, and with all your mind. This is the great and first commandment. And a second is like it: You shall love your neighbor as yourself. On these two commandments depend all the law and the prophets. (Matt 22:36–40)

These two commandments ought to be part of our daily life, at home, at work, at recreation, as we travel. Human affairs that exclude God or ignore the lesson Jesus gave the lawyer eventually meet with disappointment.

While many spiritual people integrate the voice of Jesus in their daily lives, new effort, thought, and action are needed to be part of the *theosis* concept. Letting faith in God speak to us in our work provides fulfillment instead of the *lives of quiet desperation* to which Henry David Thoreau referred. It will orient us toward meaningful work and help shatter our narcissism since it will teach us to simultaneously serve others, transcend ourselves, and hopefully encounter the very presence of God.

Some people find time to be with friends, get involved in sports and entertainment, and have fun. Many of us think of the Lord's Day and *remember to keep it holy*. Briefly and fleetingly we go to church to pray. But is that enough? Can we really keep our spiritual life isolated from the rest of our life and the rest of the week?

The way toward God requires awareness and decision to live a spiritual life. This means with Jesus as our companion, let faith and spirituality speak to us in our work and at home, teach us to move beyond ambition and success, and help us to stop worshiping at the false altars of career and prestige. Work, then, will be a contribution to the world and will have greater meaning for us.

With Jesus as our companion, let faith and spirituality speak to us in our work and at home, teach us to act on the basis of our better moral impulses and values, and help us be more creative, compassionate, and socially responsible.

With Jesus as our companion, let faith and a spiritual attitude help us integrate the many facets of our being and give them meaning and purpose. Jesus will instill in us strength and enthusiasm for work, especially when work becomes wearisome.

Many people burdened with anxieties, fears, and earthly cares find comfort as they connect with the Creator and feel his presence. At the moment of surrender and trust, reaffirming that God is in charge, we sense his strength, security, and sanctification. He is the one who blesses, protects, and sanctifies each of us. *Theosis*—our becoming divine—offers the capacity through the presence of God within us to overcome any difficulty in life, including the greatest one of all, the fear of death.

Theosis reassures us that we are not slaves or victims of a negative social system. We are sons and daughters of God, sharing his glory as co-creators, destined to inherit his eternal kingdom. The apostle Paul fortifies our faith in a loving God, when he says:

> *I consider that the sufferings of this present time are not worth comparing with the glory about to be revealed to us.* (Rom 8:18)

Thoughts to Consider:

- You have a choice if you wish to begin your divine ascent and experience the state of *theosis*. Regardless of who and where you are, already you are a son or a daughter of God. The Holy Spirit within you will help you in the process, from weakness to strength, from confusion to clarity, from fear to faith, from sin to holiness.

- In a state of *theosis*, be grateful for what is available to you; celebrate life, develop it, and share it. Jesus said that he came so that the world might have life and have it to the full. You can take on the style of Jesus, personifying him in your daily interaction with other people and behaviorally revealing the miracle of his presence.

- In your effort to attain *theosis*, meditate on the following words: Do all in your present power not to fall, like a strong athlete. But if you do fall, get up again at once and continue the contest. Even if you fall a thousand times...rise up again each time, and keep on doing this until the end of your life. For it is written:

- *Even if a good person falls seven times*—that is, repeatedly throughout life—*seven times shall that person rise again.* (Prov 24:16)

Epilogue

The early stages of writing this book were difficult. I felt like a child learning to walk. Each time I stood up smiling because I could take a few steps, I fell. Once a good idea came to me, I proudly put my hands on my keyboard, and then found I could not put my thoughts into words. Each time I fell, I tried again and gradually mastered the art. Because of the difficulties and the opposing forces that I faced concerning my own aspirations, I discovered that to attain anything of worth it takes faith in God, and it takes patience, persistence, and prayer in one's self. Now this book has become a reality.

If we are not vigilant, we may miss one of the most important aspects of life—spirituality. It would be catastrophic if we ignored the fact that we come from God and we are on our way to return to him. We cannot escape the reality that we are not just a body of flesh and bones. While our bodies grow and age, we have a soul within that keeps us alive, and it will last into eternity. It is God's gift to humans.

The peril of pursuing spiritual truth—perhaps an issue intangible to logic—is thinking that we can attain spirituality intellectually or scientifically. Truly, logic can travel with us far, but not far enough. Science can even reach outer space, but how far? It takes the eyes of the soul and the wings of faith to carry us to an understanding of spiritual realities. One can hear various voices of doubt and disbelief:

If I don't see it, I cannot believe it.
What I believe is good enough for me.
I can't change the world, and I'm not even sure I want
to change my own lifestyle.

Another peril we may encounter is pharisaism, that is, behaving like a Pharisee—complacent with appearances and external expressions: talking about things of faith without believing them, advertising personal philanthropic actions to impress others, appearing *holier than thou*, lighting candles, and being pompous in worship practices. Spirituality is *a love affair* between the Lord and us, developed always by him and our acceptance.

Today, as throughout the centuries, the Lord invites us to take a responsible stand, to be obedient to his commands, to respect and love each other as he loves us. Again and again, He reenters a broken and painful world each day and finds crowds harassed and helpless, scattered like sheep without a shepherd. He reassures us that he is the good shepherd who would risk his life to rescue even one lost sheep. Our part is to be attentive to the voice of the true shepherd. He asks us to share his yoke, adding that his yoke is easy and his burden is light.

For people who believe in Christ and in his plan of salvation, it is essential to pay attention to the nonphysical part of our being, our spirit. Life is sacred; the inner part of our self is sacred. That sacredness manifests itself as our inner essence, the divine spark, the soul that can be enlightened and nourished so that it may attain an intimate relationship with its Creator.

Nothing can be clearer than the truth that Jesus Christ, God in human flesh, walked on this planet among all kinds and classes of people, planned and gave to all—kings and soldiers, saints and sinners, rich and poor, educated and illiterate—a lifestyle of love and compassion. He taught and proclaimed the *good news* of the kingdom, and cured every disease and every sickness. He invited us to follow in his steps, to be caring and loving like him. He takes the lead:

> *I am the way, the truth, and the life.*
> *Whoever follows me will never walk in darkness.*

Bibliography

The following are helpful books that have enriched and inspired the writing of *Five Steps to Spiritual Growth.*

Booth, Leo. *When God Becomes a Drug.* Los Angeles: Jeremy P. Tarcher, 1991.

Butterworth, Eric. *Discover the Power within You.* New York: Harper & Row, 1968.

———. *Life Is for Loving.* New York: Harper & Row, 1973.

Chariton, Igumen of Valamo. *The Art of Prayer: An Orthodox Anthology.* London, England: Faber & Faber, 1966.

Christodoulou, Christopher. *The Interconnection and Fusion of Greek Philosophy with Christianity.* Garwood, NJ: Graphic Arts, 2003.

Coniaris, Anthony M. *Daily Vitamins for Spiritual Growth.* Minneapolis, MN: Light & Life, 1994.

Contos, Leonidas C. *The Lenten Covenant.* Los Angeles: Narthex, 1994.

Dyer, Wayne W. *Your Sacred Self.* New York: Harper Collins, 1995.

Fleet, Thurman. *Rays of the Dawn.* San Antonio, TX: Concept Therapy, 1976.

Forest, Jim. *The Ladder of the Beatitudes.* Maryknoll, NY: Orbis, 2002.

Foster, Richard J. *Celebration of Discipline.* San Francisco: Harper Collins, 1998.

———. *Streams of Living Water.* San Francisco: Harper Collins, 2001.

Gillman, Neil. *The Death of Death.* Woodstock, VT: Jewish Lights, 2000.

Iakovos, Archbishop. *Faith for a Lifetime.* New York: Doubleday, 1998.

Kalellis, Peter M. *Pick Up Your Couch and Walk: How to Take Back Control of Your Life.* New York: Crossroad, 1998.

———. *Restoring Relationships: Five things to Try Before You Say Goodbye.* New York: Crossroad, 2001.

———. *Restoring Your Self: Five Ways to a Healthier, Happier, and More Creative Life.* New York: Crossroad, 2002.

Mamtzarides, Giorgios I. *Orthodox Spiritual Life.* Brookline, MA: Orthodox Press, 1994.

Marler, John and Andrew Wermuth. *Youth of the Apocalypse.* Spruce Island, Alaska: St. Herman of Alaska Brotherhood, 1995.

Newberg, Andrew, Eugene D'aquili, and Vince Rause. *Why God Won't Go Away.* New York: Ballantine, 2001.

Palmer, Parker J. *Let Your Life Speak.* San Francisco: Jossey-Bass, 2000.

Rose, Seraphim. *The Soul after Death.* Platina, CA: St. Herman of Alaska Brotherhood, 1995.

Saliba & Allen. *Out of the Depths Have I Cried.* Brookline, MA: Holy Cross Press, 1979.

Stanley, Charles. *The Gift of Forgiveness.* Nashville, TN: Thomas Nelson, 1991.

———. *The Wonderful Spirit of Life.* Nashville, TN: Thomas Nelson, 1992.

———. *The Source of My Strength.* Nashville, TN: Thomas Nelson, 1994.

Timiades, Emilianos. *Toward Authentic Christian Spirituality.* Brookline, MA: Orthodox Press, 1998.